BIONIC COMMUNALITY

T0288316

BIONIC COMMUNALITY

Brenda Iijima

Roof Books
New York

ISBN: 978-1-931824-94-1
Library of Congress Control Number: 2021930646

Cover image, Reid Moffatt, "The Nest", digital painting, 2020.

Cover design by Eric Amling

Author's photo by Ivy Johnson

 This book is made possible, in part, by the New York State Council on the Arts with the support of Governor Andrew Cuomo and the New York State Legislature.

Roof Books are published by:
Segue Foundation
300 Bowery
New York, NY 10012
www.seguefoundation.com

Roof Books are distributed by:
Small Press Distribution
1341 Seventh Street
Berkeley, CA. 94710-1403
Phone orders: 800-869-7553
www.spdbooks.org

FIRE: rapid oxidation, combustion, carbon emissions
war, racism, bigotry, riots, territorial disputes
intelligence in all forms, psychic disorder
solar radiance, ravishment
burnt filaments, exhausted stars
a state of wonder and awe
flaring reality
purification

WATER: overload, dew point, drowning in data
cellular movement, oxygen, blood, body mass index, absorption
gorging, torture techniques, age of meltdown
atmosphere, oceans, rivers, lakes, forests
cooling pools, solidarity
capaciousness of being

WOOD: inference, soft tissue, open valves
menaced timelessly by sticks and wands, seeking no one's favor
resolutions, peace conferences, growing dissuasion
alive like wood and nestled
wood is ancestry
take to the wood in trouble
have died here twice over
sleep too, relates to wood

METAL: the periodic table is recorded in metal
metal will hold us in but not forever
metal is keen
metal causes brain damage
elemental depth of metal abides
metal to grip operating structures
with metal there is initiatory strength outlasting cellular function
leave metal behind, in the rock
don't hold it
don't need it

WITH ALL FLORA, FAUNA, AND MINERALS
ALL PRESENCES
ALL HEAPED AND ENGORGED HISTORIES
ROTTING SOCIAL CONTENT & CONTEXT

WITH MY GENDERS
ALL GENDERS
ALL SEX
PLANETARY & COSMIC CONCERN

WITH PSYCHIC COMMITMENT
SENSORY APPARATUS
A SEX WORKING
ABUNDANTLY CLEARING

CONTACT, I.E. BODY WORK
OPEN INTERPLAY, CRISIS MANAGEMENT
PERFORMATIVE DISSONANCE, CORPOREAL
QUESTIONS

AN AID ORGANIZATION, A DANCE TROUPE
INTERRELATIONAL TERRESTRIAL AND
COSMIC PRESENCES

AN INSURGENCY INFLUNG IN HOMETOWN
BY UNDISCLOSED TOXIC WASTE DUMPS
RIVERBEDS, DAYBEDS, HOSPICES, CEME-
TERIES, CITY HALL & OTHER MUNICIPAL
SITES, FORESTS, ROADWAYS, SCHOOLS &
BRIDGES

we went to the wall
we went to the mound
we went to the supermarket
— bearing
there were houses
there were factories
there were cages
there was stratospheric atmosphere
& feedback loops
the time has come
the time is here
the time is passing
sunlight, shadow, night
deepest dark of cosmic expansiveness
burning, exploding stars
thinking and participating in all our capacity
persons in the forest
persons by the stream
persons in the nest
this is a school
this is the county jail
this is the YMCA
this is the water filtration plant
this is a soup kitchen
this is a former tannery
this is a dungeon
this is an army recruitment center
this is a daycare center for the elderly
this is a meadow
this is a mountain
this is hometown sociality
this is symbolic space
this is here and now
this is futurity

Castle yard nihilism
choral voicings stream
through cacophonous infrastructure
historically fortified so the hustle pulse rhythm of water
coincides with the tempo of the sun and moon
distant star clusters and orbiting gravitational matter
a body arrives on a sidewalk
musculature in miniature teeming testing excavator
body reclamation catapult unsteady and civic
took a number then spun
turning knives in the fresh wounds of a butter cake
drilled through autonomic nervous system
emotional regions
this session begins with amplitude and unworking
commotion of harbingers and soothsayer impulses
an overlay of rejectionist clutter as trauma crowds membranes
a body hears a body hearing
here's proximate density feeling
bedpan clang pang of incertitude up against bulk commerce
discussed initially on a lawn gesticulating
producing lesser interactions on your lawn by the fountain (plastic)
mock swan of small-town amplitude and fray
red splotches all over sky, water, and land
shadows infiltrate, enlarging form
making contact with the fountain
contact explicit — on your lawn
signs of life (palpable)
now salivate

thunder primer bloodied handkerchief
ravished caught in slow motion
pelvic melting you thought you knew that pickup (painful)
truck impetus and a tyrant emerges
coincident to the infinite become on the verge, of earth
in this hardline 5-mile zone the air is cleared out
a small town within a chronology of hardship

we are local recall
we are fisted muster

got what you know and held it
also as known
is known as known
is unknown

saw through the horses yet not seeing
we haven't seen any lately
become rare and then contestable disclosure
regurgitate not the story or what is latent in the story

find circulatory system, nerve routes
gallbladder, liver, spleen, and heart function
zigzag contort push blood push
circumnavigate yet another civic structure
realign the country

built with the concept of terra nullius
we paid and now want to know what is ours

I found myself here as a prosthetic outside
slipstream misstep dislocation
senses burgeon to accommodate disavowal
all that is breaking under the guise of fine

embarrasses the impression of normalcy
here, this instant, this day
scrunched tightly in a ditch
uncovering history buried alive
the rawness of implication drips with tears
vanquishment was a brutal achievement
oppression is buffed to a shine
to peer at as if to render blinded
as if this reality wasn't the totalized living corpus
genocidal facts receive but a byline
now in the now the weight is incontrovertible
stumbling buckle at the gut, seize the heart
recognize granularity in soil
I'm performing for full disclosure
caressing submerged implications of
existence fettered unfettered
a rhinoceros decommissioning shadow
composed of mutating membranes
on the foothills of a mountain are fields
no one uses the term art in these parts
there's some food and hardship
jobs in a box

with every step a query of permission so that ambulation
is incredibly deliberate and slowed
every pebble is consulted
every bush, ruderal floral entity
every photon of light
deep history absorbed in the earth
is summoned as blood returns
to veins of iron lodged subterranean
magnetizes consciousness
caregiving a patriarchal dying
as follicles flake off

engage I provisionally as
an I cannot be unbound
denote I as a stand-in for proliferation
as semblances of coherence and departure
merge and regroup remaking play
infinitesimally gigantically

an intimate exteriority and a getting to know
the strangers in and of the body elaborated by many
the we resembles an I
the conventions of the autonomous body
falsify concomitant attachment
gifting selves with continuum
we come together as curved comeback
same as the semblances' differences
an I that is we comes to take a reading
of traumatic residue (ache)

when we kneel here on the soft moss
resonances of older catastrophes burgeon
relational valences yank at meaning
complexities require revisitation

become intimately conscious of streetwalking,
meadowwalking, forestwalking, gravewalking
of where a body is expected, anticipated, contested

being white no one shoots me outright
mostly where I land is private property
tiny paths of sidewalk cling to
fringe of roads for pedestrians (few)
traditionally, those who walk are poor
public lands, civic sites, and tracts of forest

focus on how much law and mortal wounding it has
taken to wrest spacetime from Indigenous nations
a ruinating eternal return
as legislation continually refers to precedent
jurisprudence as an overlay / thus outside / comes on
as power with the capacity to smother smother
formulating a plan to exclude modes of belonging
as a timeline becomes numerical

I could be mangled and disposed of in the forest
as many of my sisters are torn and rotting (rank)
reassembled by multicellular
and unicellular organisms
the tiniest beings embody the person
in a way a murderer cannot
a bionic relationship rebuilds the world
within the world
in this series of movements, I trace
femicide with ecocide and genocide
the triangle visible on currency
disposable income, a sign of comfort
and threat, threatening
every dollar is a henchman

from this vantage the chimney of the fort
appears crumbled and dilapidated
the fort is a strategic tool of enduring
settler colonial violence
tools rule
enclosure
disclosure
disposal
merge
merger

enter a force field within wedged desire
mountain and river magnetism / grounding presences
tributaries of permutation
vector of valley and grass
Cro-Magnon memory recedes at play
today aiding all functions: hips, crotch, stomach
the elderly man who is my father needs nourishment
sips from a cup with vivid straw drawl
spool kinship together holding the vessel
our fingers touch
unite familial registers
he lounges in a wheelchair, so I roll to the door
wheel down concrete steps down asphalt driveway
rolling is a continuum of motion play of healing and care
months roll by and we roll the wheelchair
absorb wind from the mountain and moldy
germinating furniture
skin is gymnasium for microbial action
space absorbs modulations of time

being right here in the now and later
hereafter week after week upon week
sun cycle moon cycle
salty days precipitate sky residue and river water

every moment a little more depth of field
with gossamer detail
partake breath

attachment and aversion are
sides of the breastplate
spontaneously stripped bare
disabusing
mergers and acquisitions

mammalian children under four feet in stature pass a swollen mass
massively breezing and seeking reconnaissance overview avenue
head of hair damp / matted due to rolling
gravel from rain overflows tributaries swollen mouth of
new developments / a flow of cars surge
past the intersection by house and road
in front of awareness and its guidelines
seeking insight

dramatic enigma seeding a diorama of time and space
one couldn't reproduce the weather like an instance
blow steam when rolling within neighborhood
unlike any gesture previously experienced
just now to relieve the imagination
let down my guard
carriage of cell a ball-like vessel and it is revolving
down the hill
spurn enthusiasm to bond with a shadow
find time to reconcile harm
the window is smashed, yet we must go on

do I really
need to go there?
you need to go there

techniques along an edge of worldly
choreographic philosophies
as the locus of sharing
we walk on our graves
as daily gesture

the body wants to right itself (parole)
willingly, bodily, financially — infinitesimal signs

fire, they go to the wall — jubilant, smirking

civic space is semiotic, now possible talk
do all communities require conformity? (jpeg)

serpent undertone wants to focus on a crucial dilemma
essential living (biocentric)
aggressiveness — we are in it — we presume to run it

they come over and say they want to
but we are crushed and slinking against the sink (hole)

do it — (ethics)
cue up / defined as corridor of existence

intervention by crawling
we don't know how to talk about it
transformation of time and labor (plastic)
aim at transformation, competition nook
of war machines, DNA structures
machine is disguised — intensification

you want me to stand against the wall
we were forced to —
we were forced to comply

organs pressed against steel
re-choreography to loosen restrictions
blur surveillance
rupture militarized silence
straitjackets sanctioned — like fear (tight molecules)
blob of protoplasm smear sick ass-sprung well

open aperture indeed, flung wide
river near anal oasis, the very question of existence
alas, there has been a lot of murdering around here
cue up — we want to
we want it (reality)
crawl — typically viewed as a dependency model
in addition to crawling and gathering information

leverage with a big white fork
we contemplate animals killing each other (sustenance)

by this point she was wearing a studded collar
by this point the highway was a steady stream of light and motion

snake remained out of sight
a breast hangs out of her red silk dress, on all fours she is
the feminine as darkness, earth, dirt, lowly, death
humidity and sexuality

the feminine as a system of representation: clean houses
forests, swamps, cesspools

sink — tis sinking — a feeling / any sense of conviction
any sense of adjoining / commanding
any sense of bonding / contending
sinkhole body patrol, or sinkhole knowing

leverage of pain in the joints, sockets, tendons
then roll away, roll into
foreplay, mailbox
my torso is lodged at the mailbox
as if stuck to it for Pete's sake
sullen this torso won't budge, daily news

frost is apparent the surfaces are slick
rigidified neural amphitheater of thick lust
beckon a call from inside the sack
bodybrain as wheel in spacetime

plunge seemlessly where the sensation nests
dig into historical concatenation
corporeal bulk suspended
shiver into flow
the moon opens a window
onto connectedness
sorrow is a ruin living like rain

brooms up our asses, yes yes asses
are assets our assets comparing our assets
then comparing our nests, nests
successful hole from mouth to anus
the flow is admissible is recoverable
the flow is regulatory and great

time appears connected to eventuality
of the reckonings that need to happen
a foregone conclusion
fights a way to reconciliation

murky — dirty ropy silk blossom that loves soil content
running micro intelligence in moist strands, pop up and respond

hydro accumulate and run-away chain reaction
a furtive mushroom fills up with cesium, sucks at disaster
we thought we could produce milk if we sucked each other's nipples
this action did not in fact produce any substance

algae and lichen came out of the ocean and made it to land
in a mutualistic relationship with each other
they synthesize and regroup their individual kingdoms
over deep time, connective interplay
crusting over bodies of trees and rocks
lichen cradle algae in harsh conditions
to survive here one needs holding
lichens eat rocks, salvage mineral content
suck as they do
pollutants are absorbed into their bodies
the lichen thallus contains environmental toxins
trace chemicals from body to body
we are connected by molecular bonds
forming social networks (amalgamations)

theories search for cohesion
areas of accepted income groups
areas of accepted cost for commuting
areas of accepted time for walking
areas of accepted time for driving

disparaging names for people from rural places
mountain fairy, hick and or hag
bandage stereotypes and topical breaches

there was a case and a point, not here, not her
run back and forth between the trees with arms flailing above head
every so often crash land with minor commotion
stare at the surrounding atmosphere
a roundabout on the periphery of sensation

look for tree line if this were iconography, she'd stick her legs here
instead, solo / not solo dancing for an unprepped public
discovered along the edges

hello — I'm dancing, don't be alarmed
hello — this is dance, outcome unknown
the nomenclature is unsure
derived from a communally expressed set of gestures
emanating from floral, faunal and mineral presences
offered to a hometown collective unconscious
exercising the softest parts
exposing vital organs
laying bare pessimism and shame
dressing wounds with river, sky, and sun
movements that anticipate need
a seed anticipates the world

stare down the crux with blinders off
semiotic evolution of selfhood
evocative of sociality as a practice
exacerbation time is living
make a case for how we can coexist together
modeling holism

the wreckage here is particular to the immediacy
of spatial coordinates, longitude and latitude
global as a worldly dimension

dwelling on femicide in a downward spiral
dwelling on nation-building, the cause of
unending grief, a worldly echo
genocide, ecocide

again, here, specifically here
the Mohican, Pocomtuc and Munsee people

displaced from, specifically this place

chronology a blood thermometer

settler colonial financial strategies
of disastrous expectation
commerce that trades in human futures
and past lives never surfeited
loosely built stone row with wind holes
embrasure in stone column
slabs of slate and granite
backfilled to the present

initially the feeling is personal and soiled
responsibility, a vital organ
after rubbing up against the sky
awareness is collective flickering wonder

I remain hidden
exhaustion, like historicism, or like theology
silhouettes property
gesticulate on a tree stump (platform)
no one seems to notice (daylight)
— observe (physiological)
in the surround
of a zillion details
sensory data merges
as I position myself on the stump

a copy of my actions is documented
cars careen along a curve
eagle codified, filed as raptor
the car repair shop adjacent — everyday protocols weigh in
could slink over there, adjust the struts
the work that un-formats as potential (energy)
connect flesh to a proximate cue
commingle
interpretation of the figure (resemblance)
internalize the sense that fossil fuel runs through our lives
chaos of eroticism + fiber + sky + fist (surrounding dimensions)
species commensurate with overarching motion
in the aforementioned regions spasms renegotiate
banality understood as brutal necessity
crashing through the day
prestigious structure and our dependence
identify with prestigious structure and dependence
in red silk rejection comes as high voltage upper thorax
neck to diaphragm
nociceptors cause flinching
dorsal root ganglia, trigeminal ganglia
heel drills into shin, head bobs and jerks
top and bottom are reversed
sky is all over the earth

peeled the scab off the wound in mid-flight
momentarily her ideas are my ecology
to approach her gaze is spot-lit inference
we study traumatic incident together
held deep in the loins
as children we were pitted against consequence

whipping shaggy head of hair (avoiding passivity)
maneuvers that yield evidence of involvement
no longer the innocent bystander
nature and their nurturer

slightly bloody and raw (ramifications)
spine bent backwards on slivers of wood
stretched out to reach toward denial and unhinge
intention from tight stricture

young pilgrim peeled the scab from the wound
that was such a bad idea (disturbing)
ideas of empire cloaked in religious fervor (economic)
look where this led any notion of us

the gas station doles out combustible substances
other animals move through ecology mostly
with limbs, wings, and fins

her ideas were of the reader and of the polis
qualities of air touching down
red silk rustling
doth see, hear, smell, and feel
doth cognate with a lineage of signs
imperatives of dreams and dreaming
red silk signals captivity
bandy about the term freedom (bowdlerizing)
right — scarlet letters
she suggests I wear a red-magenta bra
on top of the silk ensemble also red
ok — sure

I'm wearing a secondhand bra to overlap sumptuous silk
the dress might have been a business woman's attire

who is the woman who wore this dress?
can I access her through a discarded article?
I long to understand her as I attempt to pivot
on the rough stump
I want to understand exploits, my mother tongue
dirt — it abounds in this scenario
the stump was chain sawed and then hacked it is jagged
we said *really* in unison

dirt, my mother tongue
she shat on my body as I emerged
a semblance understood as exteriority
to be born and borne is to drag consequence
toward the presence of the present
gestating inside tongues of silence
to join cacophony
reproduction commissioned by the world
wishful shaking — torso, fascia, spinal cord
bearing place

jaw rattle / jaw declension
I now smile at the house
I smile at you and your house
there's potential in the aural outcome
houses, housing, smiles
adventures in homeownership / classified
come on out, I don't know you
we could get to know one another if you step outside your house
I encourage you to open the front door with the wreath on it
that says *WELCOME* and merge your body with the light
merge with id's shadow on the tough grass
while I extend my figure to the sky somatically replicating

a desperate figure on *The Raft of the Medusa*
painted by Theodore Gericault when
he was the tender age of 27 years old
conceptualize the largest petroleum operated ocean raft

the desperation and necessity to be transported elsewhere
out of a zone of conflict / terror

harsh and crappy is suddenly this pose
feel sick yet very much alive
soul pedal body
claiming a stance
then retracting at the
carceral gates of Elysium
only to emerge from the little cell like boiled meat
muse crucially from ruins
the temperature is ticking upwards as
history repeats itself
peels, is skin sensitive skin
someone sure beat us to it
symbolically and literally
too harrowing to show

she suggests flailing down the road where
all the houses were razed
her aunt's house was demolished — PCB overload
a straight line of asphalt leads to trees and eventually
railroad tracks (where tonnages of waste were dumped)
a red silk metaphor as disgorged motif
as an interior view of the body alive: crimson
the body alive: red: also, malfunction: red alert: stop
the dress was made in Bangladesh — not a local sweatshop

it is reassuring to see her focused at the end of the lane
scoring the remembering
she films so I know she's participating in hematology
she's there, dual sensuality
she's got me on record
offending propriety

peering through the curtains at your kittens
upside down body exploits view
they see me dangle / three years after the fact
now we are in custody — witness protected
coterminous, non-fucking, visualizing — look
the looking / just barely free
wind pushes at flag's edges (POW)
combinatory / circulated through psychosomatic locality
and articulative phrasings — you can say
how it is — affect county — psychonautic topologies

the illusion of an outside might emanate from / house
a conceptual framework of interior / nuclear family
in contrast with outside, unknown exteriorization of presence

the house is permeable, a membrane in a hologram
of the cosmos that flows time simultaneously so that
today is always yesterday cushioned by tomorrow
yet the house is encrusted with the collective ethics that hold
a society together, decide who lives in houses, differential
power, setting up protections and defense against invasion
the house is a set of coordinates immobile for a duration
therefore, you are where you live and are accountable
for your possessions
escapism informs a cloistered mode decorated with prompts of
wellbeing — romance ontology with figurines and props
a nubby sofa, taupe, off-set by gold chandelier
because a house is dark — requires artificial light — sun
is blocked — separation of — floral, faunal, mineral presences
except in the shape of commodity
there are bigger and bigger houses
and, one at the governmental seat
an alabaster fort / responsible for headcount brutality
flames encroach the house's becoming
fire and flammable materials correspond to take the house from the house
return the house to atmospheric intention

we worked through the night — a 52 ton mass
positioned on the edge of a hole
indefinitely leaning, sagging at its core
there was an option to buy
he said *what is sold here is land, not art*
in effect capital
is all about classification toggling on a precipice
malleable understanding in that the missing referent
resembles a coffin

anything is only part of where it is, he wrote
they treat it as a target and a splinter
I felt it was a crevice of the body
sort of neglected — a hole, yet tactile, also voided
touching there is a direct response
think of the contact not as an illusion
the method of application involved the body
this time: green sateen from the 1970's handwrought
dramatized — making a scene
the glorified, national body projected on a platform
contrasted by subordinate categories of being
that are organized along lines of race, class, gender, and species
this dance forges through the hole of cultural identity

the hole is beckoning
the abuses no longer fit

pay scale on hierarchical crash course
prison labor sourced
a vicious circle for the hole to center itself

the hole seems empty — that's the presumed nature of holes
labor rarely syncs up with income
dig all day and receive little pay
illusionistic vapor developing efforts — please share
the veil is operative

a certain amount of desirable pain
accompanies elasticity
suspense oozed — combinatory frictions (frosting)
queen-sized green taffeta prom gown possessed
harkens back to debutante balls
the mouth of the mall is closed (foreclosed)

on the same day we embarked on the mowed plains
to honor the dead, morose ceremonial againness
against the immediate actions my body takes
veteran's memorial space
reincarnating lost objects with the libido of armor
shift to primordial topics (topos)
sexed reproductions seem to be posing here
can't be refusal if advocating difference
channel weather as affect, elaborate on the name
advancing motions for your prompt response

the rule gives permission to haul in two sharks per outing
reconciled events with confirmations, enthrall the kill

flying / has flown — telluric trajectory
imagine — lawn — covert space program
reckon, body pose, flourish the dirt in language
kick dirt up to invisible vault / shoulder
this interlude was witnessed by other than human
persons

culpability, rocks, subtitles
hard memorial, rock solid
when you see flags, they indicate death
often the proud deaths
representing the sovereign
the legitimized armies
of the hegemon

fluorescent coloration
splinters glow

give off blossoms
digging below tree roots
when problematic / uncomfortable table
bury beneath a sheen of nonchalance
as a mythological construction that details birthright
sovereignty, or how we landed here as a parking lot
delivering goods to harmonic appeal as if a force of nature
braced by constricted nuance

the unmarked graves are exponentially more numerous
as the killing is wonton
the killing approaches extinction (levels)
exceeds extinction for many
gone
to bare the narrative
is
oxygenated and springs up on top

findings found finger pointing to portrait
of young girl menaced
recount the trouble
hegemonies mix with motor oil harmonics
her braces bore holes in her shins
violence protrudes through the screen

quotidian mountain stream
rocks interface elements visit
preparation to dismount the hard site
biography kindling incendiary culmination
stressor cascade rotten timeline moldy comb
combinatory ambulatory gathering
statistics scant acidified ground
whereas what if not her lauded?

I trespassed that section of spine
in the memory bank
upfront loose and tangled
climbing out was nearly impossible
rattled digits at neckline fracture
she became my inner working reuptake
I dragged her around the periphery
with all the grace I could muster
reinscribed names of the crimes against nature
wind and adrenaline
marrow coagulates inside oceanic construct

ok by you — consensus lending
agreement foil superimposed affirmative
K-hole — consequential void
ocean where we all go can't go
we all are ocean
K-hole no hole the dolly zoom the jaw shot
at once there with no space no universe no horizon
a vivid screen / an oppositional relationship
to witness to whatness — fakeness
what happened to my fur / (mine) (landmine)
synthesis fight-ness fitness
spare no expense to kill the shark
sharks represent fierceness
older than trees
beachgoer of the K-hole no hole
in the hole, all disambiguation

"it" in "witness" — the "ess, the missing "t"
K-shaped economy / all the way to z
power is coy, coils in confrontation
they want you not at all in the way you want them

who is them you want?
indemnify wantedness
metaphor like a handrail
get down on the ground now
this is no publicity stunt
this is a fact-finding mission with
intentions of understanding reconciliation

related to the heroin highway and opioid crisis
a state of affairs
forces — drugged privatized drive
dragging provisional mouthpiece
to assuage the pain thrown under the bus

now or the vacancy is replenished by catastrophe taking a form
of total dependency
it is now and never to understand mutual calibration
when body recedes into body or camouflages human excitement
a predicament of riding on the outside of a narcissist wager

come out wherever you are
strike at the heart of the ethic
strike at wonder
it is now or a faulty horizon a deep-water chasm
broken wedge of expectation
calving submerged chambers
made to look swank with body impression
made to look real in verisimilitudinous glamor

bite the head of the Tony, the Oscar
1- or 2-degrees cops fail to understand the prognosis
still wearing glimmering blue eyeshadow

still drinking liquids from a plastic bottle
hair in a bun where sky meets neckline

thrown to the ground
a cop jumps on the young girl's back
a cop shoots a round of fire into a young man's back
because repetition is structural
and apprehension is double-edged

problematic payload contends curbside
forgone mild afternoon
can't get off the ground
the law has gone ballistic
a lawn with a pool and a pool all lawns
kidney-shaped trying patrol
cops on the lawn cops on the law
omission triangulated
he points a weapon at kids, violates reality
violates all air with violence
violates all beauty of an incommensurable moment of life
a stance a descriptor a vagrant principle up against imprisonment
hush now in summer's misty light frontally before the stop sign perishing
diametrically opposed in a holster with a semi-automatic firearm
upon the lawns growing dissimilitude like stripes to wear as pageantry
lawn of illegitimacies and genocidal containments in contentment's way
harness the holster by the tree and crush knee into citizens
rely on state violence to maintain a perfect lawn
cockamamie is an Americanism genericism lock-step ordered sentimental
as bullets unload into his back, pastoral demographics are recorded
downloaded through a chain-linked fence perimeter
around the amphitheater
of crimes against humanity
tainting evermore a similitude of protective cover
and all allegiances in this time in this place sink hellishly under

fraught so hard with asinine somersaults of how to handle
a summer's situation

he modulates voicings to forge a question as language disinte-
grates (aphasia)
super-conscious of kindness and nearness changeable direct
there is a floating noun in the ether
the noun suspends itself above the ground
hovers as a body of moisture and intent
eventually the noun descends and settles
the noun is now an atmosphere
the surrounding infrastructure of meanings
engage the impact of the noun on its jurisdiction
context dissolves in the reality
of what the noun does in holding up
space catching the subtlety of phonemes and vocables
within the metal brackets of the wheelchair, prone
the body takes on the configuration of its confinement
so on Henry he goes (chairlift)
as we make directional informational phrases in the yellow kitchen
by the time we make it to ground level it is another part of day
the driveway black slice of infinity and night
rolls out a possibility as well as a trajectory and then the van
appears
and he is away, driven away
a senior center for dementia
by the train station
senses collide are abridged
reorganize
hear what you smell and then taste
open mouth fueled by lightning
feeling was never so rich

attenuated attention unending
from day through night
demonstrate tenderness without reservation
shame transforms into illuminated sensitivity
durational frequency upending mention

the mountain is grounded down, old and won't withstand
dualistic division
bedrock shows through at bald spots

when bears wake up out of hibernation, they
are groggy, hungry, and stiff
sauntering over to herbal reservations along a ridge

you go missing for days on end
which is typical topical like clockwork or organ failure
the search party can't use a full range of motion
or the spectrum of sense

pit by echo chamber
in your goat phase
at high noon
only to question
privacy
a minor offense
cleaving to opinion
as a speech act that
dangles
precipitously

delivery of bodily revolutionary pleasure and grief
into a yard glossing time with attentiveness and reflection
I wasn't skeptical of my body's surrender in the space
of ephemeral ongoingness or at a locus revealing entrails
guts have answers
the shin and mound between pelvic centeredness
probe there to integrate process
collective dying as status

every day a new beginning
reenter the language in action
heads turn to the visitor
they have been arranged to die in the ward
jostle expectancy
wilted floral presences rejuvenate
when singing begins
what they know will disappear forever
taking with them cellular archives
admonitions as chimes sound alarm

gently sponging gently combing being mindful of feeling
glide over skin membrane of consciousness
tomorrow is eternity in incremental installments
for now, an everlasting momentary suspension
real-time motivations / cellular connectivity
carefully bathing and attending / being here wholly
in a space of dying and becoming
adjusting sweatpants to comfort creature familiarity

two women and a man
one wheelchair and a dining room set of furniture
a wheelchair does not fit / have to dismantle the frame
configuration primary
care as all-encompassing psychic and physical intervention

be here today as forever
a stand of white pines the same age as my corporeal being
their torsos are fragile though they are tall
watch the wind interact with their needles
there isn't a horizon to be seen
the forest is dense and welcoming
this is our sanctuary civilization of trees
in a place of rocks and twilight

interbedded blue-quartz metagraywacke
salmon-pink dolostone, and blue-quartz conglomerate
minor interbeds of black and white
albite-spotted phyllite resembles the Hoosic
rock bed tonality

here at the western edge of the state
was the continental margin of the proto-North American
landmass of Laurentia
rock beds 1.2-2 billion years old
Laurentia collided
with Rio de la Plata Craton and Amazonian Craton
to form the supercontinent Rodinia
kiss these rocks to the lips of spokenness
with flora looking on, circulating atoms of oxygen
calcite marble pebbles within Berkshire schist
wave action carried argillaceous material
what they say is change and changeable
imagine the peaks once as tall as the Himalayas
imagine every paw print of bear, bobcat,
chipmunk and squirrel peopling the slope
hemlock feathering troposphere
snow melting down the mountain
weasels making dens in leafy berms
star matter shows in their eyes
forms of prophecy / forms of engagement
cued to neuron transmissions

calling on reserve function trim light contact retinal polemical
childish immature animal shoving the furniture up a tree
in a primordial state surpassing the horizontal mainframe
and from this vantage downhill looks grand
we don't bother sharpening the crude tools of daytime
to muster our courage

rummage through my formative bedroom now stocked with
ameliorating soft items that absorb the inner body's moisture
the notch is taken down and preserved
trophies wait for transport
this final phase of humanity is a cycle of transformation
a white birch rubs against the house bushes encircle flowers
pollinate

donated to us was this wheelchair that works somewhat
until we round a corner, we go in circles
to test the axis of the world
as insect, I spin additionally on the floor
so beautiful and fine
hard carapace and a will to survive
on the ground
bright-eyed and responsive
many names and kinds all with spines
little beetles and bugs in a flurry
graceful, agile, and seemingly indestructible
to learn of their possible extinction is to come
face-to-face with epic conundrum
dance june bug on the moist layer of earth
dance moth and fly forth / head with compound
eye, thorax, hind wings, antennae
plump furry white body glows in the light
8 million to a trillion gone
biodiversity is earth knowledge

response: coded video highlight
body suspension — molecular action, radiation, biometric shifts
body held by grasses above soil's roiling realm
I'm all over it — the ground, contemplation — hurled, off-
flow
cowering by river, rocks, the river
applied use value / capitalizations (industrial) (military)
when we submit as citizen-entity, rain wending way
possessive use solutions appear in the field of visionary concern
as sheen surface porous movement
topics intervening (coordinates)
a public hovers above the forest (axiomatic)
rules that accumulate along the gumline
with teeth the archive insists
body archive in fat squeezed revelations
gut fat wants a word, swears it wants to speak
self-dome chance in the middle of I
around and about proximate nexus
leaves defend me, floral plumage
left to ulterior devices — scramble knock dull pitch
I needed their assistance
a target and then a blur thanks to photosynthesis

continually metabolized timeframe
in afterhours of eyes
in attenuation of cellular collectivity
the scale of the physical is the scale of the cosmic

rose from scenario cache
subverted trauma in the dirt is absorbed by contact
exaggerated reversal, prone, long, knocking
behaving with relish
canines sink into the trove
stockpiled evidence and information

civilization as last resort
contamination not this flow

out here anti-archive throwaway detritus fixation
conditions for atmosphere conditions for open proposals
devolution claims marching across bodies
a notion like armor, protective gear
now become bionic through utter vulnerability
porous and transitory

open into marrow not fussy with food slurp up subject
performing hot viscous arousal
pebble morsel cuticle blemish
anticipating suction yanking dangling

lower body tilt ground reaction forces, grass, grasses
center of gravity
gait impulse, grounding soldier self
headless wired quasi sentient killing device
horse headless and tilting, angular acceleration animal
cowbell, heed, don't heed — come running
salt lick nipple navel clit swivel thrives, humiliation park
sink into stones earliest tools earliest weaponry

to come this far and pronounce the obituary soundlessly
sound pressure converts to electromagnetic impulses
and in the vestibule
there's an auditory signal related to the tempo
splayed at chamber, gated subject — torrential
conditioned to be subservient cost analysis and
bow to objectives, thrive the fence, grasses implore

encircled the back part of the supermarket
with gestures that have no words

impart the extremities the skin blood membrane
I wouldn't mind decomposing with discarded vegetables
body entry stimulus
nice and rotten all over again

proxy in sweat
rubbed sticks with legs with grass and asphalt
chemical swell
grounded ploy
rubble trouble
neck here rock hard
anus communicates through the mouth
just one long channel
sweat coded
on all fours
the fence is gone

gender trouble asserts itself
troubling the animal bubbling space
men's XXL
tee shirt covers the wounds
covers the national heartache
discovers the breach
wake up and rub against inference
sleep with dissident rebelliousness
a counterinsurgency comes on cons on

I'm more animal than definition acknowledges
ultimately floral and mineral groaning
in animal's name
human is a botch job pacemaker

a timepiece is bruised
no shoes on my feet and my knees crave
gravel to polyester a line / horizontal flare
tuck in the insubordination

commune with sentience in the form of wild
pursuit: they meet me in the clearing
at a longitudinal firestorm
the engine is off / stalled
fatal contradiction initiates degradation (nadir)
mammalian "New World" expansion
was and is a project of erasure (antipodal)

eyes peer
bunny, chick, kitten, fox, cow, pony
portrait of wolf

what is being expressed is an
outgrowth of local presences
as a conduit my voice box
around the mouth
sprout fangs sprout roots

contact at marrow, bloodletting river flow suction
graphic impact reaches limits of space (grandiose)
inseparably from now until awakening
brutal jewel of war presently centered as zenith of gravity
the troops former civilians armed and primed
relent all factions
limelight theater
battle cry emitted from thickest fortress
come home, soldiers, lie down

recondition materiality minimal postural undulation
map quest expressly — places to go / animal talking
talking rock and mineral, discoursing stream and brush

let me knot the work anon drumming butter thick
dresses engulf the state apparatus with imperatives
constructions plaintively say big thunder judicial peak
over and above the call of duty
outlaw indexical surge

jargon of the dance so hot so svelte legs all mustard
dipping into yarrow and goldenrod, scratchy ivy
pineapple weed, curly dock
a green dress becomes a green field
let loose implementation of stems
a thorny condition sun bent / swaying / swaying

a junction, two roads intersecting asphalt melt
traffic patterns and rhythms
the journey happens on a sidewalk looking at cracks and crevices
weeds of wonder reel, road shaped like a vein
occupants in a house spray paint brittle plastic deer and squirrel
near
bathing pool the house sighs butting up against the route
lumber by sweating small body deer squirrel dog
we see one another
in our plasticity got it going on
deer are decaying saying wild embodiment
gait to ambulate toward a field of repose
submerge within bending postures of cat grass, Johnson grass
sway along roadway cars shuttle unbeknownst this system
there are the stones of the dead — contemplating tombs
rigidify / corpse pose / become hard / gneiss
stone of death / stone of earth
crumbled little pebbles and rubble

a dream entanglement of living and
becoming through death / within death, relax
relax out of one form into another

tombs cradle awakening tombs
red is how the body splays in remembrance so lunge
in mourning ecstatic sober closely
begging an end to defamiliarization
begging closure opening

quarried marble effigy as upright veteran
is now laid to rest under loam sprouting thyme

funnel body into a cone — conical head with girth oscillates
bodies delivered by horse and buggy onto sacred hill of
consequence like any sign with dual associations
geopolitical contexts fight bodies, death (public art)
harkened to what the body is
heterotopic elsewhere remains assembled in repose
find memorialization based on stature
outside the perimeter are unrepresented bones
knowing is removed, removal plaintively (history)

simultaneity is best exhibited by the body
language impasse overcome by muscle fibers
the motion of death in soil's activity below human sight level
becoming at this connection blades of grass second fur
what related behaviors do we share?
is there a misreading when gestures are altered?
hands up don't shoot
what gives permission?

representative deaths commemorated
ignored in the present as ecological feature
at once adversarial nature (persons not honored)
frozen in the sun

Hillside Cemetery, established 1798
their bodies were forced into holes
they had fought / indicated by flags
collateral damage is this too, these hero tombs
murky blood chain, reflexive imaging
everywhere to turn in residual fallout
inside rib cage, afterglow death smudge
1798, the Alien and Sedition Acts
become United States law
making it a federal crime to write, publish, or utter false
or malicious statements about the United States government
rite of passage scripted within the incubator

writhing human corporeal energy
within the space of honoring the dead
to seek faunal and floral persons within the confines
with unguarded instantaneousness / mineral salience
vestigial mechanisms of the body correspond to blind mole rat
smell of burning flesh wafting
collapse on mound the stillness breathing in kind
skies that my father finds beautiful derive
from atmospheric pressure
droplets related to phenomenon
nitrogen, sodium and oxygen excited by sunlight
during the day
grand water trine peak future occurrence
flags of veterans register wild gusts of air
throat amid vague shapes accumulate in the lake

consistently menacing branches of power coordinate
cutting into fabric
impulse collective can't absolve ambushes
surveillant overhaul plus or minus high impact loads
battleground

sharpened wires external rampages internal bleeding
abandon alone collarbone emerging factions caught in firing zone
vague until impact
remembering into a funnel rendition endeavoring
tanks tossed in the air mangled
arms reach to the constellations
cubical array foregrounds charnel ground
drone fighters at their desks
within *here* somatic clearing reduced as emblem
into addenda's multiple struggles gripping
body energy disperses helplessness link
disintegrate the laws and manufacturers
reconciling a world of finitudes
Ursa Minor, Ursa Major

made in America a blank too big for that
blank too big, big symmetry groups, big dogs
big locomotion, big cows, bigger yet, chickens
towel dried, debeaked, neuter-plunged in industry

dogs and dogmas
doggedness and doggonitness
enough to induce tears to form and tears to foment
up the expression of mild irritation to blank blank
dog-plucked taunt and bracing

polynomial equidistant clusters of detention centers
and what we tend to make is
rendition *was this the intention?*
taunt and bracing internment with a name like that
torture report and binding law
someone must have sense enough

atomic nucleus-quark theory
Orpheus or another symmetry group
in fat shade prancing
pomegranates tantalize
taser pointed finger pointing at a trench
prank involuntary control
a genre of reticent civilians
alas, occasional fog
fat shade of equidistant clusters

survivalist bug out far from normal normal
normal like genre or home, hormonal
hormonally want to wanna
homey homily stripes and stars
concussive equidistant clusters, mighty quasars
shun the curb, but to look back, technically Orpheus

or another symmetry group
the hazard of running or being wrong
the wrong race, class, gender

the unicorns pleased me today
last great hope
for humanity
great white whale / hubris of oceanic scenario
delusions of grandeur, importance
motorcade, Jackie O
play with Smurf congregations and aging gnomes
ceramic deer, plastic frogs, flamingo groupings
obsolescence and probably something altogether else

plunge a trench, point a finger

wars are technically economic stimulus for war mongers
tantalizing like equidistant clusters
my wrists twisted
and then the horn prong stabbed
point a finger at the trench
bug out away from normal
below strata
bury the footfall
close all tabs

dance as a way of stimulating emergent motion nose dive
into backyard pool out of season
caress the air while falling into water
water is shady big whale glamor
soiled wet gnarly hickey neck
break landmark
tear air at tear duct squalor
dancing on a middle finger
in the swimming pool slimy grease shape of virgin

shape of virginity hickory thicket birch breech bent witches
chainsaw carving with owl
chainsaw carving of an enlarged can of Coke
a war nobody wanted
show more results
a playground is a minefield / covert operation (nationhood)
plunge finger to forge alliance
atmospheric vacuum release
backflow from war zone troubles waters queasy
owl virgin dance floor pool room version
they want cunt or freight and or serenity
they always want to dominate
plaid and khaki neckline
disturbing waters
dance not of death in plaid
get out of the pool immediately
someone screamed
I fled as a mountain lion
into the shrouds of morning dew
rain eased the membrane
feeling of flowing toward oceanic
form

endangered animals decorate the umbrella
because it is raining
cats and dogs / acid rain / Cesium 137, etc.
it is reigning on Project MkUltra-human mind experiment
test subjects bow to tactics far from *normal*
underneath the vinyl dome a body tilts to terror
as if all the blood and guts of high school shootings
create the screen to witness an explication in shards

additional suspects dashed off towards the underbrush
missing from reports
then I walk the young children home / they don't know me
nor as stranger / possible mirage
colorful petite unthreatening hair in ropes and chains
back in time / back to timing when the bus comes by
charitable "I" "am" — svelte
conjecture isotope America
conjure intentions always (incised)
thunder and wind
a durational discharge to enter the change
unswerving directional arrow with thunder above, wind below
they seldom venture on outlying roads without joining armed
convoys — imperial thrust dayglow
came for the hunting of fur
young gunners / sip tea from elegant white china
internal gardens / crisis in summer
crisis protozoa crayfish / salamanders
as in the woods fisher cats / máxkw / foxes
juveniles prowl beechnut, stinging nettle, sumac
small prey / as the children shriek in the yard, diesel bus fumes
trail behind the matrix of consciousness

solar timing, body tilted toward light in light is light
shedding the forest with a broadcast of arms
bubble and burst jagged branch sever veins
presence of primal forest benefited by feathers
wolves are denigrated, assigned kill status
wolves as pilfered bodies on the pyre, witches
land rovers, busing bodies out of the zone
triple eagle, double ducking behind bushes, thrust
men's XXL black tee shirt with wolf portrait
in this I gesticulate, moving around the lawns and sidewalk
trimming the edges of the civil, civilization

I am no more savage than your sister
canis dirus, a wolf six-feet in length that ranged the continent
from coast to coast and it was the *smilodon*, the saber-toothed
tiger, larger and heavier than the tiger of today
who dared to attack even the giant mastodons
stone age digging technology and the bionics of millennia
umwelt of animal in the eye of existence
wild by the water filtration plant wild ways along serpentine river
I repeat: I am no more savage than your sister

visible vector
immature — lash through water, dense rows of cilia
fleeing reaction and deflection — an animal swims forward
unhampered by crawling movements, same action modulators
a small animal is extinguished, this elicits the effector cue
an animal bobs in the water, she has peripheral organs
her intelligence is not centered in the brain — instead the total body
is orchestrating / engaged
I have drawn an illustration of the firing zone
the tanks are visible
the ammunition is visible
despite the convoys and submachine gun fire
despite the civil unrest
hypnagogic and hypnopompic phenomena occur
sudden brief muscle contractions
illusory sensation of movement — danses de fées
sleep paralysis as the armed conflict begins
and undertook an early example of a scorched earth strategy
by burning towns to prevent the Roman legions from living off the land
excavation project at Alesia, where Julius Caesar
put down Vercingetorix' revolt discernable as if
on the grounds of North Adams, Massachusetts
for instance, where the immature saplings indicate clear-cutting
unhampered movements of body archeology as stereoscopic effect

without map
strip clubs are a later development gentlemen's clubs preceded
cabarets where strippers danced on stage and were paid a wage
mountains of soft material formed the upper layer of strata
no wonder with conundrums centering on them
that the Etruscans have gained an aura of mystery
cut up credit card statement / recut tree
at the juncture where she had to gnaw off her limb for freedom
if you were tantalized by the sex interplay
symbolisms are not always present, but arousals are
erections the bolder experiment takes
to overcome the experiment, the basic premise of bare life
drudgery of animal existence when converted to human status
terminated either by touch or verbally
the Ganzfeld Effect — deprivation of stimuli
stare-glare, white wall edifice effect (museum, prison, office cube)

she escorted me into a dense thicket of the forest
tied me to an ancient pine tree — my wrists were bound as well as my
ankles and necklace of vertebral arteries, vines and veins
parasympathetically though the position resembled torture
as I was left to fend in the night air of inner sanctum
peaceable creatures cared for me in the space of being and event
they thought of themselves that way until engulfed in the conditions
of the forest, matted enteric, metabolic convergence

(i) the Department of State;
(ii) the Department of the Treasury;
(iii) the Department of Defense;
(iv) the Department of Justice;
(v) the Department of the Interior;
(vi) the Department of Agriculture;
(vii) the Department of Commerce;
(viii) the Department of Labor;
(ix) the Department of Health and Human Services;
(x) the Department of Housing and Urban Development;
(xi) the Department of Transportation;
(xii) the Department of Energy;
(xiii) the Department of Education;
(xiv) the Department of Veterans Affairs;
(xv) the Department of Homeland Security;
(xvi) the United States Agency for International Development;
(xvii) the Army Corps of Engineers;
(xviii) the Environmental Protection Agency;
(xix) the General Services Administration;
(xx) the Millennium Challenge Corporation;
(xxi) the National Aeronautics and Space Administration;
(xxii) the U.S. Small Business Administration;
(xxiii) the Corporation for National and Community Service;
(xxiv) the Office of the Director of National Intelligence;
(xxv) the Council of Economic Advisers;
(xxvi) the National Economic Council;
(xxvii) the Domestic Policy Council;
(xxviii) the Office of Management and Budget;
(xxix) the White House Office of Public Engagement and Inter-governmental Affairs;
(xxx) the United States Trade Representative; and
(xxxi) such agencies or offices as the President or Co-Chairs shall designate.

We'd like to manage the risk with you…

muscles — spindle response (learning)

cave painting where we sprayed painted
on the wall:

(a)   "preparedness" means actions taken to plan, organize,
equip, train and exercise to build, apply, and sustain the
capabilities necessary to prevent, protect against, ameliorate the
effects of, respond to, and recover from climate change related
damages to life, health, property, livelihoods, ecosystems, and
national security;

(b)   "adaptation" means adjustment in natural or human
systems in anticipation of or response to a changing environment
in a way that effectively uses beneficial opportunities or reduces
negative effects; and

(c)   "resilience" means the ability to anticipate, prepare for,
and adapt to changing conditions and withstand, respond to, and
recover rapidly from disruptions.

Sec. 9. General Provisions. (a) Nothing in this order shall be
construed to impair or otherwise affect.

four horsemen — three wheelbarrows
hospice of flowers — several remedies suggest themselves
an obvious one: her intense vision
grotesque and intoxicating
carried over into important theoretical
frameworks of crisis management
someone must have sense enough and morality enough
steer planetary concern / the meetings were interminable
shooting for a global temperature rise of no more than 2 degrees
planet retroactively over
thermal infrared radiation

heated oceans, heated rocks, heated air
despair

night vision goggles as if to clear a pathway
through extreme doubt and confusion

in a tiny white house where I was raised
under the velvet light of the horizon
working for a pittance
of relief / naturalized into weight
carpool to stinky factory thankful
for a chunk of mountain / purple frost
pressure from the mass of stone
educate the dawn with deliverance

fetish of fresh air collapsed lungs
a suppression of life in the form
of past tense adjudications

step here for the grilled addendum + delivery
immiserated victims of global capital + mountain air
global channels of air-jet stream (floating oceans)

gloaming on to an exuberant mirage + delivery

the garage contains the stuff of generations

namely shovels, tires and oil canisters

brooms, spades, clippers, saws

bicycles and lawnmowers

sticks and stones

bags and barrels

individuated force-mobile
selection of location of residences / walking to-and-fro
similar scenarios compel the trajectory: gallon of milk, bag of groceries
bus stop / bike route / pedestrian path: human byways
sociology tries to pinpoint why she would land face first on the cement

trespassing: private property has trespassed
as a system of inequity
precisely what is owned is what impinges

dislodge the archive from megalomaniac impulse / terror and pain
occupation front and center yet concealed as a stealthy concept
organized within a cellular medium, all memory / filtration
encounters with objects are impossible / there are no objects
there are no subjects either
curated through retroactive formation
remember slippery viscous pulsation as terminology regroups in soil
event also falters when vibing with all earth
an urge is not nearly event
how I am standing here impacted by cloud and mountain
a question that circulates as collective mandate
I is a collapsed mechanism
resolute and immature
I'm interested in giving up
as a strategy of identity
shedding I on this rock, *so long*
resume an inquiry in cellular understanding of all life
restring language around electric cables
tuned to the rights of nature

trajectory / dirt road / forest path / space between houses
main artery atomized admixtures and residue overlay
encroach the former bunker, a stone wall by the supermarket
the concerns of the day are bagged

vault now an invisible high point in the atmosphere
leave in droves, economic stream, an outpouring
bricks in heaps, detritus crossing
recuperate from shocks to the system
a crumbling infrastructure, patrolled streets
under de facto
martial law
a recovery was proposed and remains a conceptual tool
a necklace in the drawer forgotten, there is no occasion to wear
such accessories
a periphery only suggests more of the same economic dismay
power structure to clear the space
to remove the residents
to raze the structures
this has occurred so monstrously before

'twas salivating
earth was about to bulge — limbs refuse silence
earth was about to open its mouth — limbs rebel against silence
the lieutenant finds meat exotic / earth is exotic (life)
a pack of wolves / vampires / cannibals
after all, lambs don't eat lambs
after all, a kid'll eat ivy too — wouldn't you?

we live in mobile gasses on earth
continually absorbed by soil
moth lovers are falsely depicted
viciously slanderously —

a forensic analysis
shows the extent to which a mischaracterization
pins psychosis on a trans person, a lover of moths

the real serial killer is much more obvious
in the form of a system that conducts
genocidal, ecocidal and femicidal business
bumping up digits, remains, assigning female
to everything that does not comply
precariously dependent on extraction / appropriation

lamb of all archives, the absent referent could be
any missing person
100 parts of helium / permeable / speculative
Clarice! Clarice!
she will never undo but she will uncover
putrefying bacteria / decomposed organ-mineral nitrates
history thickens palpably
yes or no, Clarice?

I appreciate names strangely displacing biography

when we die and decay, we are fed to the bright blue

lambs are largely elements of air:
oxygen, water, carbon, and nitrogen

we appreciate her heroism, oh we do
her-culean, harrowing, hulky
the story is however far more twisted
and the perpetrator wears a badge of honor
riding through history as if rational and profound

fall into an oubliette in an historical frame
damp and hard-pinned Ordovician time
contained in a pebble the coloration of
ice / hard and soft / bright and dark

thought implants momentarily hegemonic
biorhythmic pulses subside, stillness in a partial cocoon
tucked knees into chest by lungs and heart
corporally in a ball wound tightly around fear
glaciation shrinkage pebbled quarried
sprayed bright yellow to indicate constructive civic details
primal brain registers deceased animals extinct animals
herds of animals / species of animals unknown to
my family, myself, my nation, humanity (primates)
one-way arrow indicator
we are capital's pets
epigenetically dictated at the DNA level
the dollar value of a family meal — incantatory

in this town no one granted
anyone permission to look at art
as art, performance in civic space goes unaccounted
for in the midst, unacknowledged treasure
must be a seizure or a

missing link one quickly notes
only the young children of the well-heeled are exposed
to the outdoors
during daytime (laboring hours) in this town
no sightings of strolling infants, no stroll
that went down laden
lead, lead again laden again
arrow indicator: permission
extimacy in answers
here lies an unknown soldier I drape my body over the mound
recover a death with reuptake bodily surges
lichen have symbiotic fungi attached at their root
the unknown soldier and this body of mine, mining for feeling

untangle conceptual markers of work + survival
the unknown soldier and a body draped over the mound
mineral content of my body merges with the earth
physically we are cooperating my foot is attached to the root

the one and the many titles of recent books having to do with
contemporary collaborative art in a global context
finding water sources together + body contemplation
across battlefields, refugee camps and dying towns

fungi and lichen surfaced / oceanic foam / made way to land
lichen have symbiotic fungi attached at their root
eat rocks, salvage mineral content, suck their needs
physically intertwined and thus cooperative —
their relationship is
called lichen xenia, the influence of pollen on the endosperm

intertwined with thicket of underbrush by cemetery's edge
mineral content of the veteran's blood merges with
welcoming microbial colonies on skin tissue absorbing

precise battle wounds and grassroots / cells house
memory / into the underworld / symbiotically channeling
mentally stroking wounded needs amassing

I can hear the person interred / can feel selves
appear / the soldier offers mutual aid / I accept
marrow where there is trauma in a thought pattern

extradition

rendition

in the emergency room the misdiagnosis is established

bite deep protozoa — displaced jungle motif

forest eradication, cell death, hosts

arrive at the stream decoding bacterial genomes and vegetation

dogs were sent in, humiliation in the form of sexualized

assault, the former prison has become a torture chamber

water from the stream force-fed

force-feed hyenas

force-feed birds

frenzy upon captive bodies

hooded and interned

caged and bred

the sky a crib, a doctrine of expanse

strain accumulates

tattooed on the edge

corpuscular feel / gurney harness

convoys carry prisoners / the facilities make up most

of the architecture / blends with ecological features

hospice planetary — the obituary is written before

death throes encumber

caring for the wounded the flooded and the stricken

care of the polar caps flood plains swamps undulating meadows

Greenland ice is darkening

unique weather events saturate atmosphere

sonic register of glaciers cracking

upheaval plentitude, participatory

a reestablished feudal order discloses bodily mode

culture dreams its own extinction calls nature
that which eradicates

rethinking what coexistence means and it is late (rehearsal)
our nemesis will crumble as waters reek (capital)
something so subtle about annihilation and
human comprehension
rock that bucket acumen for fear of value and a world
power a lost winning idyll
heighten a dream to come, crashing money
incise my dreams with incoherent suspicions of comfort
bent on destructive edges

we love one another, that is for sure
improvisation and social convention
gestures of admiration in movements that create
underrepresented feelings to come to the surface of skin

all presences all presences / all beings all beings
 / smart epigenetic spasm
 / dream a miniaturist diorama of / an end to human time
a banquet / an overloaded explosive liberation
call out to animal within ode
to floral abundance
to mineral attraction
dissolve the membrane
dissolve linguistic barriers
born animal / died, is faunal / floral / mineral
anytime you rub, variant perceptual sensitivities
the superorganism twitches
with our indole rings and pyrrole rings clinging

convert sun's photons into bio energy
serotonin can be found in all plants, animals and
unicellular beings
hexagon with a pentagon imbedded in its side
shapes of togetherness abound

/ vestigial leg / opposable thumbs notwithstanding / petals
metabolism of rocks / sand / encrusted elements
gold is not indigenous to earth

jugular on display
hippocampus, cerebellum, there, there
pineal gland / chakras

/ beneath crowns of reprise

revenge strategies that revive oceans

under hoofbeat of Andromeda / angel fish
anchor worms / arctic cotton grass

predaceous diving for cash reserve at income tower

air bases in the arctic, convection of, earthquake of

warm motion, spray zone
monetary denomination fire colored
want to want to, in turn / wait in line like twine
the rope seemed fine / the rope's final end (reflection)

configurations as notions of floral faunal mineral worry

coinciding's over destroying almost touched

category and cliff face

a prognosis of rage / sociopathic craze changes

catalytic like cinematic imaging breeze

billows, yes

nowness small fowls flew
screaming over the yet
yawning gulf
a sullen white surf bent
against steep slopes
then the landmass collapsed
the shroud of the sea
rolled on
as it rolled
5,000 years ago…
disclose nature as human / looming delusional claim
disclose to nature a separate function, motivational claim

flash
we cannot take this story apart
move

post-traumatic automatism
every name in history is a reckoning
post-removal protocol then, at a supermarket for the living
like a supermarket for the living / heads of iceberg lettuce
bobbing apples off-flowing
aisle / small fowl flew their brethren their breathing
we shall feast on the Leviathan at daybreak before the economy

or wafers of lard and dirt, for real
or tubers of dust and industry slime
or the vestigial leg of a comrade
your baby, our baby, this baby

arms reach toward shaggy branches by forest darkness
Eridanus snakes the night plateau
reach overhead jugular stretched body as stark image netted

continuously abridged / getting pulled up by the roots
concerned with respect of dirt / the archival remains
mouth looks stationary is not still, micro motion-filled
eating air and light that strike the torso dull by the off-ramp
an experience of being present as a prone body agitating facts
in broad daylight a mission to support findings in the movements
shared with the public / what they say / what is the case
rotting matter and body flailing means *come on persistence* I die here
pull down my pants like a grown animal
faux skin layers foliage ready to lose a part of the self
prismatic shedding and bonding
there's interplay, a river — symbol of surplus in a diagrammatic
session
there's cachexia, skin tissue draping
elsewhere muscles managing mobility
sputter mutter materialize, insect joints bend at mid-spine
lie down in public encourage emotional relations

play dead, liken the moment to passing
a ceremony of becoming again / tessellated
navel melts into the underbrush
presentation —
horror became the familiar / horror the familiar
living on the edge of grotesque features

in the last days of the bubble
human trauma circulates as drama
in the cellar of the fallout / consumer waste / spillage
verbal judicial inked
no longer municipal junk drawers, rivers
now normalized cesspools, waste, and debris
can't get used to / past threshold markers

now, now

now, now, a lion's mane

now, now, eco-social

now, now collateral

now, withdrawal, now upheaval, now riot, now shock option,
now calm

my advice, stay alive, remember who the real enemy is

the earth was thus called gross domestic product

you don't belong there / don't touch anything

she has become a beacon of place / she has to be eliminated

monarch butterflies segue to sanctuary

ask where we live
addressing poverty in a meaningful way
on a national scale
will get you killed
give us stamps to purchase perishables
the dance in the soup kitchen is going strong
Jared the cook knows me from the time we both
staffed the mountain (Appalachian mountain crew)
on a table I stack the entire Kenneth Anger series
of paintings and they go quickly, free, for grabs
queer milieu all steaming all extending
my body becomes a dinner roll
much of the time the rolls are considered dance
sexual flavor, cruising, consent
smoke and social anthropological inquiry

now, now, brown cow now, now, white cog now
wow, newness idle pastoral
now, now, brutal now, so real I want to be your brother
right now, we are citizens
how long will we remain in this condition?
now, for the meantime, now as in tow
over-systematized then rushing water

now, exoskeleton remains, now, behemoth, now, erectile dysfunction

now, infrastructure, now, affect behavior, now, collective interest

/ now, connective tissue, psycho-social-ecological registration

now, / methane, carbon, nitrous oxide, and ozone

now, death / dreaming / postmortem autopsy

animals and plants are harmed / action / cut / passive negligence

power to investigate touch this / feel

now, when humans deny / denial / finally kill each other

we tried to rescue you, infinite you / momentary you

dichotomous now / replenished now / malleable architecture

/ we are windsurfers sun worshipers

conflict of interest
history funded by industry
the producers, the bank rollers
desire to bend over backwards away from ironic distance
collaborate with floral faunal mineral welfare painted unrecognizably
abuse will occur — shoulders extended, buttressing wind
diaspora caused by climate change
"Kiribati will be soon obliterated, but first the numbers"
33 atolls / the floodplain / island / peninsula
a small town is masked / moot / mutating
limbs sprawl, lunge in tall grass artemisia ticklish on shins
head seeks shelter, proximity to moisture / radiating
don't know the coordinates except this was a former Native Indian

trail
route to main street and town hall
a wolf dance, a plangent identifying rhythmic motif
chest, wrists, and ankles above waist above tree line merging
black tee shirt billows around matrix, arms neck and head wobble
enunciation with body present
pulse of arteries increase flow to cardiovascular system

relating to a breakdown
organic elements strewn and settled
specifics of emotionality
to be of this small town and reckoning
walking is now the dance
walking to town through infrastructure
peopled and animaled and flowered on occupied land:
Mahican, Pocomtuc and Munsee / river never stills
sorrow accumulates as a history of harm / its global coordinates

the flood control dikes are intact
notice flood plain and where the geology increases elevation
pitched on the ledges are the working poor
closed doors / conspiratorial laws / neoliberal corruption
a word of accusatory blister / marginalization / dissenting opinions
invasion of /
formally cited as perpetrator / incarceration
cages / stripped of rights / misidentification / clandestine long-term
agenda
opaque information / this body / under oath / congressional meetings
there is no evidence / incongruity / plots / metadata / you + me
claimed by the administration / administers bodies / connected to you
/ time and duration of call / hope / acts of terror

vast sea of dumped documents blurry business
corporate espionage / apparatus / COINTELPRO

newer forms of big data collection
contaminated directional / appeasing the numbers
red silk on skin, sweat
holes cut for eyes, nose, and mouth
rendezvous to the outer limits
ravishingly exposed
close to chemicals are needles
asking the body what role toxins play
industrial ghost presence / welcome the sludge stains
my knees are caked, the zone is hot
the periphery radiates sensations
other questions arise / storm cloud ancestors
late-stage appropriation / river keeps score
compromise and money laundering
the lake is a hotbed

not every titillation results in orgasm
sexual foray thick with twigs
follow attachment with a jumping motion
adrenaline reminds me of youth

raptors under pressure, fatal feel — there are 150 pairs
song birds perished many with wings are pressured
focus in perceive a diminishing
in an expansion of the field

dance — marking out / making tracks
lucidly fluidly charged overriding normalized gaze
proximal to a generative survival motif — identity suspension
outside the semiotics of human language — self-apotheosis
a neural pathway develops between leaf nodes
climb the underside of foliage
cranium — movement imprints taxa
networks of heat and energy are voices

listening to the breathing tempo of the ecosphere
intake, release, steam, mist, sweat, dew
a fern's perspiration
a fawn's sigh
air circulates through lungs and mineral cavities
the sky is a collective of breath
holding breath / denied breath

jangle tendons
plume fuck foam
unicellular netherside

bicameral then bioengineered
the problem of evil and the symptoms of the site

yet when approached by the lawn there is awe
the sacred enclosure of property
a resolute appearance
barriers are often florally imposed
stimulate desire

standing here waiting to be handled
no matter her strength
their collective care
impersonal and legislated

trespassing has punitive consequences on a

hierarchical chain / a one-way street

seemingly few penalties for the colonizer

except the long-term effects are clear

can't mastermind the everything

then to try and fuck the stick

bark hardship

this sentence is for someone in close range

you speak of responsibility

we wrote a planet of that

no want of worry

do you care to pirouette with me?
at the street corner / fumes / beak to pavement / protrusions
when Kim Jones performed *Rat Piece* in 1973
he initiated the death of several rats
he intended that the audience focus on
the horror and death of war
namely the conflict in Vietnam, Cambodia, Laos
perpetuated by the United States
no one stopped him from setting the rats on fire
there was outrage, the rats died
unknown quantities of Agent Orange and other chemical toxins
were dropped on Vietnamese, Cambodian and Laotian civilians
the effects continue to proliferate
his performance demonstrates hypocrisy
and something else
rats were his spiritual guides
the disparagement of rats is commonplace

he was covered in twigs and mud as he lit them
he splashed lighter fluid on the rats and applied
flames

the Vietnam War was how I recognized
as a teen
US imperial catastrophe as the preexisting condition
and legacy
as a continuous reality
as racialized horror
and ecological disaster
you have my soul
everything you want

naturally magnetized
what came before I cling to / lodestone?

humanity smiles when striking down

in about 20 minutes, the rush hour of the small town
I agitate at the embankment looking up at tenements
then legs give way, sprawl
mud covered body, cohesive sediment
this performance is free
you can stop me
to wake up out of the construct
humanity is a ruse
that bruises
impudent
try to remember the understanding
commonly rethinking redress
somatic delivery / form of incubating
self-by-side of road
query the self of personhood a mode of articulation

it is time for the rat's funeral
conducted as somber ritual
retroactively and immediately now
mourning tragedy vestiges make sober
this river is noxious discharge lymphatic
water is self-expression, water is key
clarifying contamination
effluvium envelops happenstance

neighbors swaddle us shoulder to shoulder
when dawn breaks, ambient vocalization
east is opening sending up a flare

he is still alive / we wake up to the reality of finitude
not a unique experiment because many white men are living
into their 90's
at home, given care full-time by wife and daughters
we are attendant with care that uses all our reserves
disabled and forlorn, his body caves in but not totally
corporality, an organizing principle
memory is slippery and impressionable
do something and repeat the gesture
each iteration is both new and ancient like breath

he calls out through the night
penis in urinal, least of concerns
fraught with the diligence of timely matters
what makes you tick, surprising and surprised
compulsively at the sink and imagine, no shower for 8 years
hand towel around the stomach and armpits how lovingly
sincerely an old man
toasty in the cocoon of elderly predicament
meant in the kindest of ways, he's the softest soul
in the living room I perform Houdini
and then Fred Astaire, Freddie Mercury
hand clapping is involved
my father asks me about the dimensions of poetry
vis á vis dance
when the truck bashed into him, I was the first
loved one to enter the emergency room
he wouldn't let me leave intensive care for a week
my head wrapped in a turban to block out lights and constant
flickering
machines / when he regained consciousness, he inquired
were you in the accident?
required at the hip, like soul, no dad
break away legs

ambulate body to place of contamination
contemplate the PCBs initially by sitting still on the mound
endocrine signals abound glitch secretes impulses
grown over and nondescript, there is no indication of the tyranny
of discarded substances washing up on the shores
dumped clandestinely
transformers, capacitors, coils, semiconductors, integrated circuits
variable timing proximity fuses: pre-war and wartime industry
the road that leads to the factory passes by the cemetery
Veteran's memorial mausoleum
on the banks of the structure do I perch
Swan chemical company
environmental persistence, bioaccumulation, aromatics

according to EPA estimates,
approximately 1.3 billion pounds of PCBs were manufactured
through 1976, and 93% of this
volume was produced by Monsanto in the United States

during periods of high activity or weight loss
PCBs are released into the
bloodstream as fat is metabolized

significant quantities of other hazardous contaminants
such as trichloroethylene, toluene, xylenes
and vinyl chloride were also found

the literature is always sobering
statistics come from a white paper drafted by Elaine Denny
"A Snapshot of PCB Levels in Hoosic River"

ponder the available data before walking through a filter
accuse body of didactic doom sputter will forcing fate
channels open / consider stratified treatment
the town is an archetypal case / to be cured

dumping grounds, living room, dumping grounds, living room
dumping grounds, living room, dumping grounds, living room
dumping grounds, living room, dumping grounds, living room
dumping grounds, living room, dumping grounds, living room
dumping grounds, living room, dumping grounds, living room
dumping grounds, living room, dumping grounds, living room
dumping grounds, living room, dumping grounds, living room
dumping grounds, living room, dumping grounds, living room
dumping grounds, living room, dumping grounds, living room
dumping grounds, living room, dumping grounds, living room
dumping grounds, living room, dumping grounds, living room
dumping grounds, living room, dumping grounds, living room
dumping grounds, living room, dumping grounds, living room
dumping grounds, living room, dumping grounds, living room
dumping grounds, living room, dumping grounds, living room
dumping grounds, earth, living, dumping ground, living room
dumping grounds, living room, dumping grounds, living room
dumping grounds, living room, dumping grounds, living room
dumping grounds, living room, dumping grounds, living room
dumping grounds, living room, dumping grounds, living room
dumping grounds, living room, dumping grounds, living room
dumping grounds, living room, dumping grounds, living room
dumping grounds, living room, dumping grounds, living room
dumping grounds, living room, dumping grounds, living room
dumping grounds, living room, dumping grounds, living room
dumping grounds, living room, dumping grounds, living room
dumping grounds, living room, dumping grounds, living room
dumping grounds, living room, dumping grounds, living room
dumping grounds, living room, dumping grounds, living room
dumping grounds, living room, dumping grounds, living room

take a break at Site K and contemplate toxins
feel into how our bodies morph
grow aware of chemical agents and cell mutation
innumerable elaborations / frustration can be a site of contention
an elaborate theme / leaky drums wherever they may exist
sympathetic nervous system rails against synthetic
conceptual underpinning, spasms as such surpass

in this case / foul play / horse dance / dirty dirty bodies
eventually the hospital was able to discharge them
the care they got did not meet basic standards
their fetuses will not survive / should have been given
this information
several intimate bodies and a source — dire conditions
drinking from the river, stuffed animal overload
remarking where it is possible
door-to-door campaign of the not-now-always
greater pressure on the regime
no-go newness doesn't disclose function
one symptom of many repetitious failings
my anger is directed at the upper ceiling of communication
it is clear how much Angelica admired him, the pirate
he had the audacity to be authentic
pigs licked the body toward the sacred
this was an idyllic scene in the scheme of things
after all, memory aborts trouble slickly blankly
feigns alternative versions sometimes in sometime space
dexterity takes the form of tree limb upper corporeal registers
growing toward the sun the mountain of accumulated histories

who goes there?
totality does away with anthropomorphic mirrors
pace again to Veteran's Memorial on Brown Street body rigor mortis
changes in muscle tissue after death — cells deprived of oxygen
rigidify symptomatically as cognitive dissonance informs posture

there is an invisible kennel around my body
what industrial farms use to house animals
bars grow into skin, sure death
I lie prone, an oversized hormone saturated sow about to
be tased / farrowing crates / gestation crates
cannot turn throughout a lifespan
steel rails fuse with flesh
artificially inseminated
deprived of sunlight / grass to roam around on
eco-terrorist if one were to film the scenario and care
pitiful and pathetic who looks / can't look
cars pass as usual, as per usual
their velocity seems unidirectional

having walked from Site K where 55,000 50-gallon drums
of the substance was unloaded onto the land
to the Hillside Cemetery
contemplating toxicity and extroverted cruelty

on one side against gravel and the fumes of emissions
heels locked into L-shaped spikes
the neck is thick and no longer malleable
belly up and twisted into a painful knot
needed this time to relinquish all claims
dogs were upon me, as were the dead
now is time to roll over if the restraints permit
to be tasted on the heels of death, mortifying ambience

abduction occurrence shelter rain if you say candy man five times
did she perish?
she is gone no longer there no longer home
pull the wool from her eyes with the longest blade of insight

why women go missing the way women are erased
blip tree line edge of habitat shattered windows shield eyelids

I remember her as a missing person as my senior
baggage of a beating heart she is plural vastness faltering specter
she, absorbed by a sea of infinitude
because she was discarded
her murder goes unsolved
an unexplained external organ
home boarding in gut membrane
public identity bears witness
to the course of her life
narrated as evolutionary status
unintentionally an icon
of mundane terror
serially everywhere
even the smallest acts
of daily life
bring this home

tough meat, tough to relieve tensions and locked positions
night is coming on and the old folks will need me evermore
still being this hog in bondage while staring at a stone structure
a squirrel climbs an elm in the grove by the 19th century markers
tough to meet the meanings lingering and becoming
choreography is merely the thought of excavating time to scene
making my way here, recorded in cellular proximity
a dinner plated corporeal form is not audience
now and again consumed

the remediation site is down the road called Brown Street
brown and or superfund
intelligence evidently diminishes
in contact with aromatics such as these
a local concoction for national consumption
grease the wheels / scale up
proprietary formulas match a chemical chain
grapple with the standard
local realities merge with global stakes
Monsanto sold to a European chemical manufacturer, Bayer
the company's first product, the artificial sweetener saccharine
industrialized nation state, how much
poison is the threshold?

2013: Monsanto purchased Climate Corp for $930 million
studying the culpability charts
timed to bowel movements, you don't want to be off

where détourned genetically modified corn
to the bone of the crop morphs briefly into a gestation phase
taken by new substances a preparatory act of war
of which corn is always
implicated as a staple normatively mutated into poisonous effect
that can be shared with all the world's people in a faux act

of generosity, ultimately a suicide mission
or a trojan horse

I do not know Clarice —
but the Hannibal Lectors do exist lick chops in our backwoods
hogtied tidy tighter combustible damaging
bottomless basement quarters when there is only breast milk available
or what comes out of the taps
rancid putrid ankle bondage why not take it out on yourself?
Hannibal Lectors, your wanton eyes, a crucible of narcissistic
outboarding
by this I mean:
animals in society change pace as gallantry
the bend toward equanimity
stumble then turn, trip then float — on a neighbor's lawn
so thickly shadowed is the house as I stare up from the ground
my chin on the stone entrance way, shins facing chimney
and look at their pet mimics fancy
I have become a witch
even if you have not seen this performance
with your watery lusting eyes that express
ropes around the jugular
the performance has an endurance of eternity and a day for shimmying

go into the dead girl's frame of reference and become myself
within her ecosystem which is our economy
forecast for all tomorrows and heartbeats
her archive is my repertoire my body is never lonely
as a performer specializing in the art of mundane neighborly relations
here I am plainly and like trauma dance protects intruders (I am they)
something radiant is evident as a social mandate

once motions are set into action
while dancing clueless not looking for clues feeling / feeling signs
no critical distance detective work / to be the dead girl
writhing on a flat plateau of grass where no one would step
onto not even the mailman who occasionally sees me
performing here and there along his route because I tend to go
from house to house or sidewalk to road to lawn
to footpath sprawl / markers as ambient footprints
with clairvoyant rebel energy boosted by exposure
perform for anyone who will see spontaneously
seismic you can't control nature
no goal nary a patrolling feature bursts at the seams
a false impression momentary in our industrial military state
pony up comrade

deterritorialize anatomical rearing — condemnation / slight slight

brace for impact

move away from chain of being into congresses of total communality
— to approach her death is to approach
a hatred of nature that resounds in culture
thus, I ask the underbrush
the weed-wacked tangle
please reabsorb me into the whole

rearing pavilion
rearview mirrors
primates in abandoned garden of occupational hazards
my sense of relief-styled repetitions / occupy wonderland features
proliferating at the expense of other fauna and flora in general
is it a downer to pronounce something as end-stage, dying, terminal
buckle up bent maximization of revalorized
quasi-intelligible meanings

you think you understand / then the body
determines what could be surveyed
they knew how to make perfect circles, perfect squares

adept knowledge of coordination with the local grid
cranium atop manhole cover and the sewer groans with muscle memory
one segment of the night sky Big Dipper Little Dipper
ecliptic plain configuration
what happened here 5,000 years ago
500 years ago, yesterday's yesterday
anthropological probe / earth mound

it seems as though they may have
served as a precedent

the great finalization hadn't yet been built

what we have here is municipal water flow / regulated flushed
out rushes
exploitation colonizers in canoes paddled here for fur / timber /
land / labor
insidious forms of acquisition

spasms notational — blowout hole also ethereal magnetic
electron energy — kinetic frenzy
inevitably this means the children will want drastic change
chilling effects, corpse sucking glow, high definition
Acheron / Hoosic / Cocytus / Lethe / Phlegethon
converge at a marshland, Styx
Oceanids group with wetsuits garlanded in trellises of seaweed
circle of discharge expands into a bloody helix of merit
npe / possibility of life

eventually a mayor ineffectively wipes up the outflow
preliminarily a governor spreads more —
encouraged by corporations
causal nexus therefore the dance needs to be
corporeal excess + excrement
residents, please look on, this is an event
point at the river and recite after me,
little baby don't you cry
we are going to make your waste fly
don't you worry, it is on the sly
your big provider, my, my, my

mutations appear in cellular structures

it is called river and then grow silent about it
get dumpy dump into the river call it an enlarged
colon there is refuse all over not biodegradable waste
and accompanying nutrients see here industrial effluviums
get taciturn around the dump the river is seething
the river saturates dirt we call this the dump
municipal dumping ground and below
is the cemetery / the body dump don't get all up in arms
placid by the company / objectionable funnel
longing stringy body goes nuts / scientific
also look at this communal wasteland
gorgeous radioactive features the land looks gorgeous
persons are gorgeous though filled with tumors
hyaline vault overhead / give the river a break
don't be bored

nature bore a hole in me and filled up the cavity
the mountain is where to place thoughts
generated around issues / how to accomplish this
must take body up mountain
deposit thoughts generated around the issues
the duke then fondled several victims and
designated them whores
in the YouTube video Hurricane Irene sheds voltage
flood control chutes channel volatile water
barely containing mass
motley motley
headlong bedsheet / body supine
breathing sounds
reverberate and moan
tension toward / spinal emulsion
personhood loses all seeming coherence
matter bunches at conscription
no sympathy or compassion for the transmogrification
we are forced to behave as history
camouflaging survival

still, in the sense of care
simple gestures comprise the day
cycles of necessity correspond with attentiveness
every request is a grace
reassurance and light touch are radiance
preparation for death with each breath
vulnerable with the setting sun / cooperating

hills are alive
sound resonates with hourglass
reflections, we found you
along the many prodded mornings
and continual structures
of time in a conceptual sense
I began to wonder
if my participation was a mercy killing or other catalyst
the lineage of this body and now servile positions
minced organ dwelling
look out the window to nature under siege as defined by
past cultural markers a speech to the Romans
"since nature has ordained"
civilian body production machines
dying is nature / the deadly play of signification

yes, mom, as affirmative as is possible
admittedly the discussion has a heroic undertone
traverse anticipated logic of competitive exchange
with whom you might ask, well, symbolism and belief

behold the archetypal body of the father
marrow of his bones
speaking imperturbably while we meet on a small stage
to confer the details — vague, I know
that's how impending conclusions can be

we are safe in this room for the time being
the laundry will be done in succession
bodily fluids like rain and condensation
we could use a Hoyer lift for transporting and assisting
not premature, need-to-know basis
mutually assured destruction and care

sadness to fury to sadness / fury modulating faded
grief and joy simultaneously
experience in a snowdome / mice run around, it's their field day
graham cracker crumbs galore represent a forest inside us
they race over my neck / barely notice in a dream state /
the moon is caked
pronounced / ocular bearing down pressurized /
silhouettes scurry
creatures / side effects of medications are rather surprising walls
and floorboards shaking bed is shaking / frankly unacceptable
and as I think about the off-flow heading out pipe channels
to rivers and the few remaining fish, I discontinue
the allotment for the old man / no sense in adding
to the mutagenic-effects platform / my father does not need
side effects affecting reality
guilty cover / recycle metals drastic drastic times
annoyance harness ill-filled construed as saddle
questionable cultural figures ride atop horses
pompous aggrandized / enjoying conflagration
eyes and ears of the convoy RPGs moving from
one target to the next
volunteers stay to neutralize IEDs
alarms sounding in the remote landscape
an ecosystem nary a bird what of disappearance / losses?
human layer / run out front door / dig hole / examine soil
sticky brown no worms now few worms worms no more
insert pacemaker for weeping do not weep due to

shell-shocked recognition
here is an indication the worms are not included
in the friend network — they are the friend network
worms, subterranean haruspices
divining the entrails

it should be noted:
no internet here, and no computer
in this house on the foot of the mountain
sputter few antennae towers / passing
sympathetic dementia laced
with childhood flashback climatic changes

a social world fades —
this obviously is a social world
friend connections dissipate as caregiving encompasses
the whole calendar of hours saturation cooking cleaning mowing
sorting clipping bill managing calling feeding singing
basic language retrieval performing theatrical skits
amuse household head wrapped in turban operatically
try every synoptic connection with chopped rosemary
the plant grows outside, helps to stimulate our brains
a TV is a sculpture in the room a urinal placed on top
appliance pained to have to insist on this and make
commotion is trivial is / surround and echo dispatch
a narrative that overlaps and sounds like sandpaper
worldviews notwithstanding please take cover
the least of our problems is a problem nonetheless grotesque
so close to the dinner table spews out vitriol
I plan to dance all over a qualification of rhetoric
disquietingly vivid, mobile / demarcation sizable impasse
stream gurgles / challenge brain centers / stare
at a high school photo, big hair / ruffles / stripes
adolescent boyishness as girl
ravens fly in circular patterns in the cloud-sky
choreographed electrical charges are lifelines

violence of town and nation

pharmakos ritual involved beating an old man
dressed in animal skins and driving him from the city

Ides of March

to be fox wolf

spider caterpillar wasp

animal woman feminine masculine

gendered misgendered

to be roaming

in a men's XXL black tee shirt

in red silk above the knee green sateen ankle length

homecoming queen working around the clock

wolf of necessity and thinking

banished and exterminated

here in the perimeter

here is the perimeter

arrived at the wall and the wall proved to be
a partition that proved to be
a series of veils membrane-y clotted cells fibrous before a body
anticipated the wall body lie prone / null / non-participatory
body realized wall as temporary unification / brain-blood

rebel fibrous bodies of complaint / we were rallying
collective embodied actions
ἔνδον endon "within", σύν syn "together" and βίωσις biosis "living"
bodies decried stranglehold — yet we have the moves
the occupiers shaking the storefronts of the maniacal
we have another tongue we lash out said storefront of oppression
as we calve upon the leg of austerity / integers
the uterus our architectural construct is flex walled upon death
we birthed calving with a spike in population
bodies burgeoning from continent to continent
all converging on last available resources / overhaul
from navel to pubis stripped of grease
mining filaments / greedy eye of bulging proportions
in limbo limbic lament oracle oral ocular
felt myself into a cavern and relieved the tension
mental masturbation surely malleable crowdsourcing, see
conning the dusk, conning the factory, shutdown production
especially chickens being foamed
what good can come of it?
at the wall a headlong image of stasis / total shutdown
rotten swimming pool / political force behind the construction
of the vast concrete and steel separation barrier
that snakes through the Southern border
walls are growing skyward with the thrust of insular rage

history flanks subcutaneous layers
protrusions scarred and severed

chemical from the coal plant drips into drinking water
protestors roll over in unison
black box coupled with green gelatinous orb
non-equilibrium systems
plush snatch crowdsourcing rebellious fibers
cluster bombs explode on concepts of community

give birth to many-headed hydra who will champion an end
some say humanity is a hydra, not in a good way
take the list, grind it / spasm
grub the eternal present

chunky spasm / pains of love on a need-to-know basis
blanking out in the eternal moment disposed on pavement
am animal might
as if animals have no anticipation
as if when they are alone, they almost have hope
they is death by another name / signals other

how long do I have to shutter-shake here?
before the Parks Department ushers someone to
take a look at the debris
nudge with a shovel handle?

cardinals in a tree above sightline
send songs into the twilight
blood red silk merges with feathered crimson
past and future fold into one another
horizon becomes scarlet

the sun comes out on the silhouette of a fallen body
borrowed slice of sky on a hunk of loam
you humans hiss into
the face of the dead woman
she offers an understanding in friendship

while dead in a sense / rehearse a poem, "politics, sex"
bring language to the spasmodic circumstance / this is permitted
language must arise in the enacted present
hormonal response to psycho-social dirt
memorized lyrics are already parasympathetic nerve responses
a litany — verbiage grounds the incoming obstacle
brings forth a longing for stillness
space has the ability to stretch — expand
nowness is like that — a rubbery dilation
nowness of the cars and the trees and at this juncture
a bond with regurgitated verse

diagnose now and the corpus will will itself to death
longevity has a foothold in crime
moving is repeating the future — dancing the not-yet
a future of infinities, eyn sof to think of one is nullifying
hwæt / we gardena in geardagum
air triangle, valley of the self and the non-self

crudely hiding behind a curtain of doom
that shares nuances with joy and exuberance
demonstrating agility in pronouncing presence
 — the horizon of senses leads to telepathic valances
wild grape and lily of the valley intermingle
wild aster comes after leading to frost
scramble to cooperate understandings
hear with sight, love with breathing

conformity — that form of labor
labor of appropriative balance
labor at the station / substitution
genetically altered — they feared invading substances
perhaps posing as safe the sameness appeared benign
mass-produced alikeness / allergens of same
fields kill fields
office plants leer at the administration
administrative details deny the plants nutrition
laborers do not receive the proper protection
a revolution in the fields
you can bite into a green salad and come away with
nothing the lunch break amounted to non
insipid noncommunication
clamoring for nutrition
mass-produced substitutions
neutralize dawn

Miley is and is not Miley is not a green salad
Shankara became one of an estimated 125,000
farmers to take their own life
as a result of the ruthless drive to use
India as a testing ground for genetically modified
crops, dying supine drooping in the dust
lawyers kick corpses and scientists smirk
bodies here care about farmers there
the video will go viral
doctors immunized
shots for flu virus
the antigen requires 1 million sharks
to be killed
bland is motto bland becoming dawn
sacrificial language
again and again
sacrifice zones
nary an opportunity here
retrievable time + space
fall prey on a timeline recharging dimension
interaction software / grief seeing (distinctions)
suburbanization comfort station a bastion
dance for the food of life
a repertoire of scenes presented in ceremony
down the center, turning the body

lodged into the stream of the poem
infiltrate tongue to fist assay
communication through external device
confluence of meanings rush headlong
body rounded out like a boulder

memorized is mesmerized glitch glow superimposed
performed with dire moderation
shoved to the side by a moraine deposit / recollects
all exceptions that dislodge from a central ideological now
maw jowl tugging / immediate suppression
as the subject flails / goes around to make a point about
a future tense that congeals in embassy light
body senses outline / terminology sovereign
wake up to pejorative speech acts
now can be a rule to live by / maybe except today
wag your tail, tale, telling spinal conundrum spitting
now is liberative instance / now is binding
now begs questions / seeks erogenous zones in
primary fields — distinct areas happen
local calling and said hello at disconnection

you know that incontrovertible sensation
an affective dissonance / like when
your comforter is hiked around your hips
violence hovers over your dreams
gaseous, material, on the brink, pressurized
the products are tainted
the biome a somatosensory mall
there's an invention trampling
that somatosensory mall
armies of inventions
trampling the mall
the love is never stronger
vertigo has a secret

sacred commodity + birthright
baby grooming fine

baby reflection pond / baby pouting on golden ceiling
deliver the fetus to Chronos because he's the personification of time
fighting repetition as the nuclear reactor core destabilizes
distractions are endless and my thighs ache
hemorrhaging conceptually around the tautological center
uterus sheds a tear some mucus
glistening cum sideling along
occasionally tiny echoes march off to the bus stop / implore
eye / parent's guns and trophies, insignia
in an infantile state / yawn at the horizon
dance thematic at a slow-moving pace
feeling out maturation along a timeline
from the womb

moving space bodily / baby's name is Blue
baby's name is Ocean

baby, raw, once babies display, baby raw
what happened to baby?
remit Teletubbies
raw baby remediation lesser on babies, lower threshold, babies
the infants are gone, reservoir
infants can't be born / hormonal ceiling
Holocene finally / humans are sterile and the other animals reproduce
a fantasy in the form of uterine mutation
other animals succumb also
anthropogenic, lithosphere, baby
nomenclature for baby, baby husbandry, baby you grow just fine
corn potato soy wheat
bearing witness to the close encounter
foist baby profane data + veins
come out, play
baby gateway
ensconced, the known world
reflexively

erect wands sexploits river water circulates amongst us
through bone structure, breathe through mental prosthesis
humiliation, contempt
contempt of the world, cages, slings, harnesses
chains, synchronized swimming, dunk heads, partial asphyxiation
violence and surrender, debasement, kink, beauty, s + m
limits of consent
smoke, sexual flowering, cruising
amidst world trees spreading across safe haven
landmass biomass / feels good / feels uncomfortable
nebulous shelter for departed souls clinging to thick foliage
mayhem melts down into childhood
lubricate glands / diaphragm, punishment, escort, feeding
beauty / bury me possible safety net
more adversarial, fending institutional hegemonies
audience as a performing body, sexual favor arriving
organizational misbehavior feeding satisfying diligent host
homogenous reproduction and towering inferno
becomes their animals so they roll over
become mineral and flip
and again roll

roil angle tangle symptomatic river
mother comes to watch me drown
impossibility / water is sluggish, murky sink stones liquor store
somewhere zone of significant consequences property owners lead us
across the field over grassy man-made berms constructed by
The Army Corp of Engineers
to film 2.5 miles of river lined with concrete
that makes up the flood control chutes
designed to accommodate a 500-year flood event

diligent host / beauty s + m
limits of consent
escort animal prepped
universe exposes imprecise quotidian sensation
imprecise digressions, of dying and perpendicular motion
what we'd like to frame as living organisms
careens in charged episode actually
whatever happens to the we hereafter
is a fantasy of living and dying

high contrast magnetic resonance imaging

red silk obscures blood / circulatory system

as does obviousness + shy cowering by the curb

there goes the mayor and a city council member

I stop by the police department and make an inquiry

the impetuous for movement is always at its basis
an uncovering of missing persons, young girls, women
the ongoing crisis of colonization imposition
that takes the form of genocide, displacement, ecological
collapse

dumped, heaped, nature
there are folders of data
resting in vaults
in the cellular structure
as a meaning of our town

hug willow, collect breath
encircle with arms around

trunk the birch does so
every tree is a directional feather
a congruence of life force and place
summer crests on the crown of green

chew on purslane roll in clover
collect wild mint cinquefoil bladder campion
hurl a rotting chestnut into a field of sow-thistle
buttercups reveal the sheen on tomorrow's lips

humans depend on other animals and flora for their survival (function)
the life of nature is stripped away by economic forces
capital's all-seeing eyes of stealth can down a rainbow
let's go to a meow rave
dash down staircase
fang out by the seashells
a billion years old
tugged by glacial erratics
feel good / fell good

outside the operating condition away from the motherboard
pitch an image of how we came to pass
fetish / world paying transaction an unbroken line (ascending)
brute is being around and present
capable of triggering an oncoming crisis
insurgency stalemate dressing
black box / insurrectionary tendencies
flinch of red silk by flag motif again cars gas off
participate one and the many / all client countries
an animal can take to heart the weight of words
can litigate cost value, can jerk off (self)
if the body is repeatable, generic and computable
if then, when not mapping the process itself
plant lore, oral histories, memory maps, narratives, photos and

other anthropological details smolder as a kind of abject love
all filters down and the traffic is baffling
gatekeeper set of terms inured to injury
at this time, wolf performs 0 and 1 ad infinitum
induced vigor, wolf as a resumption of animal
implicit wager / human is a botched
categorical assertion gone amuck sump coiled
tributary tests impressions to lick and ingest the murk
of stone's bacteria / a polemical exchange between
homo sapiens and demarcated *all others*
dialogue presents the lien, an instrument beyond property

referee score pitched to canine lost zones of habitation
engage end numbers in a chemistry of vectors
primal language unrelenting mediums
hunger is a complex rite
tributary, a leg flashes, blood to valves, all living creatures
condensed into matter condensed impressions
we are locked in a void we are coiled in a forest
detachable body parts and water evaporates
the gatekeeper scores the competition
where 0 expresses hardship and 1, infinity
prey upon larger numbers, larger populations
categorical playbook / instrument of holdings and security
clap on, clap off, strap on, strap off
wolf expresses system collapse of total pressure to infrastructure
we have a medium *comfortably warm*
unrelenting scorekeeping game warden master of services
the universe is expansive as is the question

anointed with the fat of wolves to avert enchantment
see what happens to we / borrowing time splurge

snatch viewfinder / skin in the game / continually skin
150 people like this

a patient reports in a moment of lucidity or looking back
that they sometimes feel *as if animal* or have felt
the sensation of embodiment
a patient behaves in a manner that resembles
other-than-human-animal behavior
howling, chirping, clicking
other examples: crying, grumbling, creeping
19 people like this / thumbs-up / smiley faces

ecstatic
feels as if selfhood is floral
cellular regulation of dirt, wind, rain, fire
membranes bloom and wilt
we bear seed and seek sunshine polish metal
quiet in human terms reverberating with tremors of earth
with rotations of spheres crystalized into mirrors
no one notices

connective motions gather sensations
collective action groups / townhall referendums
glass domes / sidereal mountains / transitioning seasons

guzzle conniption, plastic suction / how to remove a diaper
3 people like this

Athena's owl / owl — women of war
Neith, Eris, masked and sheathed
the wowishness of the universe plus howling utterances
into the receding future of expansiveness
wail and keen swimming in a fire /stáaw
lunging toward destiny's adolescence
a prismatic dawn on a shore of rocks in the
shape of roses outlining possibility
seek identity in flora and fauna
in many faceted gem streams
deep-throated response meets heavy body of water
landed
moored
cast ashore
we scream relentlessly into voids

universal claims — realer the graves — class action
grievance / see everywhere how treaties are fake
continually feverish and overwrought
integumentary system complaint

conglomerations
served to obscure, to aggregate power, to evade responsibility
social cooperation — living tissue, decay
muscular, skeletal, reproductive
animal-always, animal-ready, animal responsiveness
growing thorns gaining height rooting into the substrate

mutual appreciation in the form of a running tributary
watery plunged sensation
find release in the gentle murmur of cellular

liveliness in water
energizing a field of daisies
honey of the field mouse's eyes
iridescent shimmer of a hummingbird's wings
the way we scurry in the thick weedy tangle
sniffing interiority as a pledge of intimacy
gathered on planet earth
materializing afterlives / isolated yet
simultaneously wholly together in planetary housing
two we's and an I all over continuum forum dispatch to system
pumisoo, Mohican word for both she and he: that person

split horse hairs, whale visions, rooster cries
we see an I like the center of time
there are bees and moths
splinters in the deployed lanterns
light refracts as a galaxy of implication
slop the run-up on empty with a
hyperstitional coalition of rock fervor
love on you earth dirt river
cosmos is oceanic
objects are paradoxical

the dog of time pitchfork canter laced with mercury after-crave
any semblance to human is speculative, we've unburdened the
mass, the massive body signage, bondage, turf implant
unwiring programs and last resort paradigms
indicated by the spikes in goneness unknowable
flash how it feels to be a terminator
to be livestock replenished
caretaking around the pain
dogs of the animal in motion in deliberation
carrying on over cloud cover
as twilight descends the animal is secreted
ocean compression and endless body spills
edges are dissolved
animal highlight
animal awareness
animal forever
light is diminished
water spills over, heat is a harbinger
and who is subject to this authority?
rescue / an epistemological critique
cross a proscribed boundary where the forest once was
now an emergency living space

wolf personifies "nature" + "the wild"
harsh, restricted, coded, circled
hunted, killed off, disturbed, mobile
territorial kin, fierce, irregular
converted by civilization, docile, trapped,
leashed / do human's bidding
defiance slain / roil that feeling
the wolf dress proximal to childhood discovery
responds to the girl dressed in red
woke the dog in the uterine tissue
blanketed the results of defective consequence / bubble numbers
when trying to lift the tank off the explosive device
now I'm undoing a daisy chain
got a globule internal vision sputter heart valve *on go*
expunged replied with the proboscis
jutting straight into the flower
yet the wolf was unseen in a terminus
such must be repeated for future safety
disturbed mobile vision the use of drones to kill wolves
0 to 1 explanation funnel
just one minor 0
just one minor 0 in a funnel hole
funnel hole angle attribute
which might have a slight reactivity
sugary exhalation dripping jelly
excite hole a minor 1
sportive arms and land mines

ice caps sea ice water heat waves heavy rains coral reefs fish
many other creatures teeming dead zones habitats
acting the part of the antagonist
without knowing gestures arrive at conclusive ends
creative disorder in your divine stubbornness
arched and supported structurally in a diegetic hush narrative
oceans coastal communities cars power plants demise
of many other creatures, organic matter arctic soils civilization
greenhouse gases desertification
starvation crop failure refugee status militarized borders
plastic residue pharmaceuticals harbor harbingers
of that which evades corner imposition
death squads terminal vacuum
cruising militia future selves
bear a relationship to larger political struggles
inexpressibility end zone craze

therefore, conducive to demonstrate motion
sensation at a resting point
grave / shrouded vantage
internment site cemetery buried emotion convert materials
regeneration wait want to become
wolf regulated civil and or evolution of dumping
transmit ruse scruff indigence bleed seeping contaminated haunch
coiled to bear relation all tangled cut up minced as decay
eugenic stereotypes: wolf
brink of rib + focus

wolfish imposition at water's edge by an off-flow canal
spurious all-group interplay referee gone amuck
transformation all the body's organs burgeon
without the pack lone wolf prank on local civic order
born in heavy wonder born at a fast-paced overload
undersong understory undermoment understorm
theft as suspended animation uncontrollable force
outpaced by naming and terror
blank unblank distribution / burden of bodies

this is also an indication of the past, past state
what to do now with tendons
nubile, there is a snake in the road, tis a petite female body
in a taffeta dress the cop stops to kick it
may I suggest cream with your tea?
may I suggest other snakes?
this is a microcosm of cops, of snakes
we are maturing
we are inverted
the cop flirted with the mechanical snake
inverted significance so that the fishing boat appears
two dimensional (modal)
you can see the canoe and the man in the canoe in the same breath
you can see the cop and the snake in the same instant
the cop is older than the snake
the snake is nubile (we don't know if the same is true of the cop)
the cop is not human as one would expect (suspects)
a microcosm of inveterate travelers up and down the mountain
the snake races the cop in the snake's mind this is the experience
they squawk, commune and joke about the inverted mountain
in the town the economic sentiment bled to the mountain

the river is polluted with the sentiment of the economic situation
before you know it the snake and the cop dispersed from the roadway
the canoe and the man in the canoe vanished
the river with toxic silt is still where it was / was a minute ago
the snake is a young girl though not a virgin
inundating landfills with unresolved imagery and spasmodic outlay
the snake has jerked multifariously and envoy

if you can, then you are free to stay
if you cannot, then you must go down from the mountain
the cop said I'm on a beat, I can't stay
the snake deposited the cream in a precipice blunt workmanship
float medicine body delirium
after language before
sieves audible now real
feel snake-wolf quite animal posing as human for the time being
at this time leap to the intersection, leapt at the total loss
allocating truth dogmatic disciplining caveat / lot
/ empire-driving doctrine
sum total / again finding 0 to 1 over and again
actively lengthening the body
townspeople approach / the snake-wolf is somehow invisible
reversing a predicament of vision
guiltless legs in arms and neck in neck
close to river
convergent river legs to the snake-wolf blow hole by the stream
no townspeople today
I'd like to meet up with you later
what does the snake say to the 0
and or 1 and or townspeople?
for now the snake is on their own as is the wolf as snake as human

to clarify how this operation takes place is to describe transitory
atmosphere
dispatch to the river for a fact-finding mission
sensorium declared in a narrative of inception
definitions of species and acts of military conventions
come now, wolf
return in the mellow air swoon with trees in spacetime
reprehensible in unison now talking about the monument
the mayor must agree, though his ancestors
commissioned the bust of the man on a podium
staring out in space an emblem of power

a wolf would have been preferable or
unborn girls
unborn in space elusive and open
the consummation of humanizing alibis
might not make sense unless one considers
civic space from the point of view of other than
human societal structures
during an expansive collaborative production
the principal dancer (snake-wolf)
gesticulates to the net debate, space envisioned as reciprocal
moves stimulate considerations
a huge impact is necessary in the field
train to be conciliatory circular function over time
corpses below surface dimension recall reuptake
dynamic over time
time over time floating the surface tension
the body is a conversation piece
once owl-dreamer, once corpse, presently snake-wolf manifestation
muscle / body containment, series of mutual cells salivating
corpses digest the dancer, in turn the dancer ingests corpses
cops come through history and out the door they will go
dispensable trouble, they must reabsorb in amelioration

in place of cops are a crop of digestible motifs
0 and 1 in plurality merging with singularities
her body is an owl mourner for loss that occurs in the present

switch the playing field rest supine a rendering of human flesh
a chalk outline signifying the dissolution of capital M
Man, a hulking caricature bearing a shadow of violent particulates
snake knows pathology, warp this way wisely

whereby the body enacts the mortgage high bearing payload
linked to a transaction that destroyed
how inertia comes in the form of heavy metals in the bloodstream
metal restraining devices sanctioned by law

the body rears up momentarily bratty braided buoyed blunt
plugged body covered with plastic a body bag a panther
with features of a wolf not receiving attention in the forest
with *a sense of themself* as a wolf she felt that when she was
wrapped in plastic gravity and the earth's pressure equalized
she might have been gutted and abandoned already accessed
left by the killer in the dense underbrush or perhaps found
later by a hunter later by the authorities dead
dead now wrapped in plastic or maybe a plug furnished by industry
the body is unclear in the clearing features are unclear clearing
mouth jaw they move gums teeth grind against water
forest is jelly on the back of corpses *it isn't about her*
gnarly fallen trunks sensitive footwork avoiding jelly
rather engaging jelly acrobatics oceanic rift
in cables to murder memory
jelly circumvented around the scene of the killing
a viscous substance oozed, biometric qualities

not unlike something from ducts and valves drips out
forthcoming honeydew discharge foul fermented sweet

muscle-spindle response
release of the deed in the dead zone
harvest blood flows to the brain as heat dissipates
enteric nervous system responsive
induction in the high court
esophagus extending down to the gluteus maximus
reap a circular structure / falter / float on ether
sex is all around us the vegetative canopy mates
intense in coloring cool in action the pineal gland
represented by roaming peacocks
bowed over twigs scatterings hips splay
into the rock dirt of burial (zero degree)
memory as effigy hemispheric and global swarms
the subtle body the gross body the sublime body
camaraderie as muse unquarantined body, mirthy earth
direct predatory behavior at the law / institutional context
mitigate deleterious effects with leaf stomatal apertures
plants implant plans of plentitude and sometimes poison
dicta concerning dissolution and change animal license
of imagination arms are swinging in orbit
bodies being the best fantasy and real actants / real
circle again around the trunk with delicate footwork
tippy toe dunk cool rain luring
fleshy disruptive experience / for once an abstracted body
as key understanding
shattering the illusion of ease crouching
by the boulder with buttocks against trunk
flourish in this minutia working with exploits of death

feedback from soil biotics / elbow throng
calves and thighs crave plant residue
redistribute morning dew with spitting motions
summer goal: unmitigated thrum in the eddies
work up the insurgency / the village of contention
work on the verge the swaying commences
during the time they worked there they circled mind
squat down instantaneous succinct
feeling range of reportage in whipping skin against encounter
full-on dark cloud rural stratosphere
buzzing iridescent sun one and only
or universes upon universes

Earth what to do with us, use?
patrol living sanctuary the campus of resistance
cops are employed by the state to serve some us
the us of houses of epistemological space
intrinsic political organization
camped out by domestic policy
crying into glass
while discussing the project of the world
they think like money
and use us / finality
degrade the mission
this totally matters
as does here-ness over and again
disaster melds body ecology
forms of rebellion the body takes
cops don't sense the dialogue
locked into cue from deep state mandate
state of mind — psychotypological

each cop an accessory of violent intention
colonizing with automatic weapons
suction assimilationist white holes
making here incapable of love, hope
and transformational resistance
fire is made of intentions

sprawling carceral state
body is a social apparatus
lockdown inside and out
trapped in digital proliferation
and heavy weaponry
we ate what was thrown away

— is no exaggeration we foraged from the garbage heap
our source of commoditized agents
our source of starch and hormonal farm surplus
discharged into the waste of civic removal
we repurposed junk + spent labor
while sweeping the streets and wiping the lenses
epic certitude slipping on cobblestone
to do this now is breaking a law (forage)
do not perch, plea or plead
do not tremble, rage or fight
succumb to totalizing amnesia

Tanja Ostojić flashes her crotch at the United Nations delegation
expressing condemnation at national checkpoints
on rotating billboards moving from bare subject to bare object
over expanses inhospitable to human life
border crossing is fraught
with more than bureaucracy and diplomacy
there is a sentence that resembles a sentence
a sentence that resembles an organ, etc.
our historical nature collides with animal
our social attachments are captivity studies
captured around the chest
primates sit to discuss
humanity's fatal flaws
built out of racial and gendered
entitlements / inheritances / violence's
snare set
forked stick
ear tagged
radio-collared
numbered
classified (lexical)
examined the teeth

scruff of neck muzzled
anesthetized
release hold
photograph the escape
clamping hands around muzzle
flick a quick jerk backwards
breaking the neck
wolf pitch stretch hind legs
broken animal front legs
heyday of hunting
sound of gunshot
aerial killing
run off quickly and silently
hunt, pursue, attack, kill, eat
you will repel the expansions

I was not the one who spit on the cop in Sherwood Forest
but I'm willing to take the blame
do you know where that is Nottinghamshire, England?
one of the queen's royal forests she appeared in my night-
mare bareback no underwear or underwire stripped down to
the corporeal business of riding at breakneck speed
the state authorizes cops to kill people according to a mandate
cops can kill spit that out
this was a performance or a book let me think harder
because reality came upon me like a loaded gun
reality is droning overhead snipers in combat gear
the word bedlam comes from the Bethlem Royal Hospital
of London, the oldest psychiatric hospital
warped logistical quandary pathologies of the state
repetitive compulsion of the serial killer
the state apparatus wearing pathology's riot gear
roses by the body bags
disaster agencies typically have reserves
of body bags both for anticipated wars and natural disasters
authority law free range
straitjacket and kettle our rage
I repeat the sonic image
language is not distinctly human
but the valorization of the epiphanic subject might be
the subject is on hold
the subject struggles to breathe
in the final analysis expansive power is a pretext
a very ominous concept floats by
stratospheric fat hotdog sky

FEMA camp weather declares something unending
a context for strategies of thinking
mobile-not-knowing response
information fodder destiny oracle talking heads
the phones they confiscated
monitor the tiny act of movement
to get to this subliminal present
and find the realm of daylight
the contributing behavioral factors
— to say queen —
and then survey randomized selective
human qualities down to the crown
survival competition theme park
I'm no different than an animal is somehow obfuscation
being fully floral faunal mineral

factoring in the dialogical project of unformed freedom
the original dependency model failed forfeited fleeced
double bind or double blind
mute to the mute button mutability for bottled water
the camera continued rolling
our semiotics drag our corporeal conditions on
one unless unlessedly unleashingly ones
temporary positions glommed on topical fences
beneath it, what?
what of what ontological charisma of meaning sutured?

immature, she died before prime number possession
before infiltration before harassment took leave

come upon three faces in the shrubberies
a protector, a menacer, a liberator
ask the serious questions / bend at the knee
the hellscape is our challenge they say as a chorus
the generosity of earth is our fate

voluntary
multi-hazard early warning system —
vagueness deteriorates
impugn all animals
all public protest has been banned
feel facts in all organs as vital information
from 1970-2012
close to 2 million deaths and US $2.4 trillion of
economic losses were reported
globally as a result of droughts
floods
windstorms
tropical cyclones
storm surges
and extreme temperatures
alone
while being altogether
provocative

— at COP 21
there is a state of emergency
delegates from 195 countries

discreetly sequester around elegant tables
discuss terminal futures
deliberate the survival of people
attempt to imagine continuing generations
generate 250 opinions
— the decision to forgo
a formal treaty is
partly to assuage
the concerns of the
world's two biggest polluters
the United States and China
old and weak
hashing algorithms
our compromises pale
prepare for failure — bone / clone
condone
done
one
on
one

there is a point where adaptation might no longer be possible —
permanent loss and damage
doubling times, lubrication of flow
goodwill rhetoric stems present anxiety
only fractionally
who are they to decide?
foreshortened —
protected from admonishment
aspirations are nice — targets voluntary
sequestering carbon, methane

climate justice can't wait for governments'
intended Nationally Determined Contributions
is failure or suicide, mass murder
sue the commons for disbelief
failure to agree
the 22nd Conference of the Parties
to the UN Framework Convention of Climate Change
Marrakech, Morocco
Your Majesties,
Your Excellencies,
Your Highnesses,
198 member countries
loss and damages
weak target
didn't cut
was cut
Earth Information Day
why it matters
concept to practice
real world necessity
here and now
life on Earth
steady and cheap
well-lit corridors / information booths
countries were urged to continue
scaling up their financial contributions
towards the pre-agreed "$100 billion a year by 2020"
empire's heyday

the now is a prediction — is tensile
a suspended opening in real-time
you can feel the commingling of futurity
gale and guile synchronicity with vectors
bodies — saturated inner lives / rational predictability
they'll have water
a glass of water
water — an infinite proposition
to maintain water as gift
the water is a glass agile
clear, held — molecular
the glass cylindrical vessel explodes concentration
one glass of water on a planet of happening
proficiency compels the reckoning
the prompt —
open action seawater
presently in the dense forest of hometown locale
or at a FEMA camp
fluid gestation — seawater / saline
liquid action
open action as in a glass of water
hard to come by
unavailable at the site of disaster
the president finally airlifts potable water in
in water days after hurricane
how we watched in suspended animation
water to a disaster of water
inner lives perturbed by water
going through synthesis
within flesh vessel
seawater glassy, rising

from here we proceed into cylindrical channels
read auguries in rainbows / institutionalize demise
kickback bashed out mainline thought process
into a redefined formlessness, we lose ourselves
color spectrums illuminating synchronicities
to be beyond within surpassing utmost scale
every jungle, ocean, river, tributary, field, and mountain
burning the entire archive of sentience
what goes up in smoke reigns down as infrastructure
don't believe this manifestation as claim payment
all proliferation
all pulsation
planetary / galactic / cosmic

again, another meeting of minds
— COP 23
delegates elect Prime Minister Frank Bainimarama, Fiji
as President of the Conference
raging infernos
tepid on the inside of the conference room
vast domain of carpeting
root and tuber
crops
almost 70% of the water used goes to agriculture
energy and climate conversion
progress on inter alia
Non-Annex I Parties held in abeyance
local communities and indigenous people's platforms
article 6 mechanisms
ad hoc working groups
Subsidiary Body for Scientific and Technological Advice

Subsidiary Body for Implementation
events and initiatives
language to exert transformation
trees, sun, moon, rivers, mountains, minerals, flowers
sonic effect of aroma, touch of sound
image of thinking

canyon allure / tissue / at fold
water thickly brink mechanism / lips against teeth
paragraphs overlap bodies / level of soul-spirit
a mode of consumption / attributes
equatorial waist deep make what you can
with the stuff at hand

most of what we remember is altered

it may be a maximum limit this wandering
as if a forward trajectory
by making the costs spike upwards
your life, downward spiral
impossible to view outwardly
we are engulfed evocative, at bone density
and nuclear considerations
get well greetings cave depth
envision a field of oppositional possibility
varying at the —
bodies as crowded phenomena
rallying
the cries are severe

the number 24 is a powerful diplomatic envoy
companionship, harmony, idealism, family

I quote as follows:
global knowledge on the interconnection of
climate and health
executive summary
image of parched earth with carcasses
decimated cattle scattered
blazing sun, unrelenting
skin of earth
crust of world
a COP 24 Special Report lists:
undernutrition
injuries
cardiovascular disease
respiratory illness
mental illness
infectious disease
water-borne disease
poisons / loss of habitat
poverty / displacement
conflict
age and gender

fiscal tools
micro-prime logic
smokestacks billow
executive handshakes
mitigate the laws
what do nations want?

the COP 25 happened on the heels of mass
insect death and bee die-out

so tall the tale of capital divestment
so fraught the spine of policy
trial by ideal / trial by proxy
survival instinct ridden of hope
phenomenon of avoidance
phenomenon of attachment
no longer dancing / head to wall
rigidified / stationary / braced
continue in a neutral tone
disposable life / sacrifice zones

burial grounds are overloaded

policy, policy, policy

is strong enough to reflect itself

floats before her

change has taken place

HEC: high earning countries

fires in the Amazon, Indonesia, the United States, Siberia, Lebanon

cut off by flames
bushfires
trapped in cars
there is no end in sight
circumstances in which they perished
embers still falling

eucalyptus trees contain flammable oils
explode
just explode
absolutely beautiful, now aflame
"are you safe?"
"yes, we are safe."
quite heavy trees
always had been green
to prevent the zoo animals from succumbing
to the flames zoo employees took the
monkeys, pandas, and tigers home with them
Mallacoota, Australia
scorched earth
seared score

slight fallacy to cordon off the day into quadrants
other animals are shot in the war zone just as humans
foliage decimated, minerals ransacked
similar to an industry harvesting profit
today will increasingly become framed
by unlikely possibilities — by shifts in financialized futures
by symbols of value that no longer exist
the dam is our glass of water in a disaster
holding volumes
suspended capitalizations, parasympathetic nerve endings
above horizon lines of deceptive screens
water will guide evocative understanding
the core identity of mineral sanity
our bodies well up in anticipatory awe

animals unite and signify togetherness
flora reorganize communal space
mineral reality is prime reality

capitulating the worry
capitulating to cascading inference
and low dose radioactive sanity
expansive eventually

we've taken a stance
active / is statement

we received a surprise visit

from happenstance
fate propositional

we must be precise
enough to elicit
in a locus

semantical
locomotion

the industry of extinction is maximizing a computational hold on
gravitational horizons and juices downward trends
to pulverize all spectacles
wow, they are said to say

woe, they are said to say
it blasted out of us with propeller quick numeration
they have stockpiles of consideration
they have a catch-all of exuberance
industrial outpost megalomania
high winds are in the forecast
a caravan of Escalades expected
their worsted wool affect is reigning
splintered ceremonial elements
rain down on the operative distinctions
cloudburst midday
cloudburst pre-twilight will give way to something
drill to the epicenter aquifer
ventricle, calf muscle spasm
gossamer longitudinal arc
Escalades to the valley of inference
the disaster zone is the region
in the brain
the totalizing matrix

sensing heat / predatory die-off
the glass of water has not melted
predictive of molecular contortion
the seeing eye relies on liquid
tragedy's conceptual modulation
teems with the death drive
sacrifice a party of one
cut off the fractal denominations
we predict the financialized forests fall
we haggle an adherence to gift + exchange
this stand of trees is industrial

this holder is an entity of
non-sovereign liquidity
please breathe
motion sensor flicker
please

wind on strong masseter
stretch legs hold sandwich board
trees resemble lodestones mark death and life
replicating evil self-suspension of presence
all summer taking to the streets
protesting the violence in our names
Ferguson, Standing Rock, all surround
so many a-monitored
vortex towarding maverick mentality
maxing cues on compliance
wind will not avow
wind over
wind beyond
we'll wind
walking backwards unrefined
stride for strike
civic space comes together
different selves — elongation
caressing global disposition
dispossession we stood up again
recovering a narrative
gripping knees and legs
blood over
windborne
situational

landmass
terrestrial flight low to the turf
carry over and on
realm of commensality
earth
earth
again
earth
over and again
earth

AFTERWORD

This text is a choreographic account of somatic involvements in my hometown of North Adams, Massachusetts between 2010 to 2015, with after-effects that continued to be written in until 2020.

Emergent forms of movement I'll call dance were performed unannounced in civic spaces, in the forest, on waste dumps, in cemeteries, in people's yards, and around town for spontaneous audiences that came upon my body articulating in zones and transitional spaces. Experiential data absorbed and operative in 360 degrees generated language. When performing, I wore one of three distinct outfits: a men's XXL black tee shirt with an image of a wolf on the front face, a red silk office dress or a green sateen ballgown. The garments affected the way I was able to perform and elicited a range of divergent responses from onlookers.

During my childhood, in the 1970's, there was a spate of murders of young women, several of their deaths remain unsolved. The violence the women endured, and the underlying genocidal history of this place (and nation) have merged and resonate. The violence clings as a second skin for those who encounter this space.

The grief of these undermentioned, and or occluded histories are part of my orientation in the world. It became palpable that the town's residents struggle with grief, consciously and unconsciously. The traumas of the past communicate and relate directly with the traumas of the present.

Through non-normative gestures and more recognizable forms of dance as modes of interaction it was possible to uncover the dimensions of trauma and conflict and touch upon the way social histories intertwine. The physical and psychic commitment of dance generated responsive resonances, motivated language, and intensified the traces of unending liberatory struggles that intersect gender, race, class and ecosystem. I found my bearings by reaching out to the lifelines all around.

Tiokasin Ghosthorse, said, "the center of the universe is everywhere", an active situatedness. Silvia Federici's rebel body as an alternative to the hero encouraged a way to realize connection. I was motivated by Édouard Glissant's understanding that "Imagination is shared, can only sustain a common surge; it is nonetheless a tributary of silence, which is individual. And the diffuse force, each can fix, but it must stem from a generosity of all."

I spent several years as a caregiver for my father, who was disabled in a car accident and had dementia (he died in January 2015). My mother also relied on extensive care after she suffered an accident two years after my father sustained injuries. Creating exciting movements became a fruitful way to access feelings and communicate in alternative, dynamic forms. Emergent movement became a necessity when normative movement was no longer possible. These motions fed into the dance lexicon I generated as a disruption to our habituated expectations of what the world is like and how bodies participate in the world. Regrouping our energies through dance eased our sorrows. Dance helped me deal with embarrassing and sometimes excruciating scenarios. Dance is initiatory and roving. Dance foregrounds bodies in environments, as environments. It is a mode of presentation that dislodges entrenched codification, exposes, and pressurizes the abstracted tools of meaning making. Cues arise from submerged social realities; the body's engagement amplifies signals: visceral psycho-social meanings with all human and other-than-human life and presence. The gestures can be understood as moving out of incommensurability toward intimacy of interrelation, recognizing that all human and other-than-human life participates in semiosis and in doing so creates habitats of meaning and history.

I became convinced that we can say everything we need to with our bodies, sans, for example, English, a tainted tool of colonization and now globalism that has ushered in hardship and violence at every turn. What would it mean to communicate somatically without the props of the grammars, syntax and diction of state sanctioned languages and instead insist on a vernacular form of communicating that involves the whole body without shame? The first lesson in caregiving is to do away with shame and be present to whatever comes up. This is also important when negotiating the facts of violence. I focused on young women's deaths and the fate of their memory — dumped in a forest or in a hotel laundry chute; forgotten, ridiculed, and destroyed. We understand that the ecosystem is treated like the body of the disparaged: without rights or representation. These histories took place on Mohican, Pocomtuc and Munsee land where settler colonial violence aimed to decimate and displace and then ignore people who lived here, (and continue to) caring for their families and the ecosystem. Histories leak into the present, are the present.

Somatic responsiveness in the form of mental and physical shifts occurred in dynamic forms as I relinquished my alliances with historical "Man," a universalist subject position that has populated the Western imagination since the Enlightenment and forced the world into its image — one of the most detrimental effectors. When it comes to sentience, "human" is an overarching category of being and the ultimate ploy used against others who fall out of its descriptive valence. "Animal" is a conceptual marker and symbol used as a tool of disparagement, ranking life hierarchically. My body slipped out of the human into the faunal, floral, and mineral returning to "self" as a collective of others responsible for one another.

Although this text resembles poetry it is an expression of changeable forms. The work necessitated undoing the stricture of genres of language and relation to embrace raw impulses and facts of body and presence of many means and modes.

In the process of feeling out life and death and their afterlives I have become devoted to the immediacy of living presence in all forms, moving out of exclusionary status. All flora, all fauna, all mineral presences.

The witness is a participant, the participant acts in relation to embodied history and geopolitical bearing. Historical material conditions often preclude certain realities from taking shape, denying their form. I became interested in superstructures, like the law that imposes quotidian rules. Who can go where? What are the systems that deny others through punitive measures? Who is punished? Who is exempted? Who is rewarded? What role can I play in truth and reconciliation?

Conceptualizations of nature / ecosystem, race and gender derived from so-called Enlightenment philosophies and extended through Western models of industrial mechanization, capitalization, incarceration, and extractive labor practices have created the catastrophe we are now living.

We regain connection in the underbrush, reciprocating energies with all presences, convening with the sun, paying attention to forlorn and disparaged narratives, flexing our bodies, and contesting monoculture's totalitarianism. Justice and futures and the civics of multitudinous floral, faunal, mineral assemblies unite!

NOTES

COP, depending on text sequence refers either to a constituted body of persons empowered by the state to enforce the law, protect property, and limit civil disorder and all of the dangerous and repressive connotations such a body entails, or COP is an abridged acronym for the Conference of the Parties to the United Nations Framework Convention on Climate Change (now in its 26th iteration, postponed due to the pandemic) and eludes to the power of state apparatus' muffling people's needs, desires and expressions as well as the evasion of responsibility for the catastrophes engulfing earth.

Page 10: "Intimate exteriority" from Jacques Lacan's, "this central place, this intimate exteriority, this extimacy which is the Thing." Chapter XI, Seminar VII (The Ethics of Psychoanalysis).

Page 52. "Someone must have sense enough and morality enough" is from an essay by Martin Luther King Jr. Christian Century 74, February 1957. I engage this phrase as a refrain and choral response within the book.

Page 85: "The deadly play of signification" is from Zakiyyah Iman Jackson's *Becoming Human*.

Page 91: "Moving is repeating the future: dancing the not-yet." is from Erin Manning, *Relationships: Movement, Art and Philosophy*.

Page 104: The Mohican word, *pumisoo*, is a word for both he and she: that person: https://hilltownfamilies.org/2016/05/25/htf-307/#:~:text=%E2%80%9CPumisoo%E2%80%9D%20is%20the%20word%20for,for%20the%20Native%20American%20Festival.

Page 115: The phrase, "assimilationist white hole" comes from Elizabeth Willis' review of Fred Moten's books in the Boston Review.

Page 127: "Almost 70 percent of the water used, goes to agriculture." Dr. Jan Low:
https: / / cipotato.org / press_room / blogs / cop23-highlights /

Information about the geology of Western Massachusetts originates from several sources, including:
https: / / core.ac.uk / download / pdf / 19716924.pdf

Videos of some of the dances performed can be viewed on Youtube at MrBrenda9865432.

ACKNOWLEDGMENTS

Thanks to the abundance of energies and presences that make expression possible: floral, faunal and mineral abundances, water, fire, air, sky, earth, the cosmos.

Toshi Iijima, Laura Woltag, Janice Lee, Tyrone Williams, Susan Gevirtz, Will Alexander, Julie Patton, Soham Patel, Geoff Olsen, Metta Sama, Gabrielle Civil, Erica Hunt, Selah Saterstrom, Tammy Fortin, Anna Gurton-Wachter, Ian Dreiblatt, Karla Kelsey, Maryam Parhizkar, MC Hyland, Jeff Peterson, Carrie Hunter, Eric Sneathen, Vidhu Aggarwal, Angel Dominguez, James Yeary, Nicholas DeBoer, Adjua Gargi Nzinga Greaves, Kimberly Alidio, Roberto Harrison, Stephen Motika, Ivy Johnson, Jamie Townsend, Maxe Crandall, Diana Cage, Julia Drescher, CJ Martin, Jill Magi, Linda Russo, Megan Kaminski, Aja Couchois Duncan, Katie Ebbitt, E. Tracy Grinnell, Alan Davies, Jared Fagen, Erin Fleming, Charles Theonia, Sara Jane Stoner, Angie Hume, Saretta Morgan, Jennifer Scappettone, Judith Goldman, and many more friends.

Endless gratitude to Reid Moffatt for the cover painting.

Thanks to Eric Amling for the cover design.

Gabrielle Civil, Erica Hunt and Selah Saterstrom, your words mean the world!

Some of these sequences appeared in the following publications: Academy of American Poets, Prelude, When Eagles Dare, Elderly, Diagram, No Deer, http: / / www.aperimeter.com /, Argos Books, The Colorado Review, Bettering American Poetry Anthology

ROOF BOOKS

the best in language since 1976

Recent & Selected Titles

- THE COURSE by Ted Greenwald & Charles Bernstein. 350 p. $20.
- THE RESIGNATION by Lonely Christopher. 104 p. $16.95
- POST CLASSIC by erica kaufman. 96 p. $16.95
- POLITICAL SUBJECT by Caleb Beckwith. 112 p. $17.95
- ECHOLOCATION by Evelyn Reilly, 144 p. $17.95
- HOW TO FLIT by Mark Johnson. 104 p. $16.95
- (((...))) by Maxwell Owen Clark. 136 p. $16.95
- THE RECIPROCAL TRANSLATION PROJECT
  by Sun Dong & James Sherry. 208 p $22.95
- DETROIT DETROIT by Anna Vitale. 108 p. $16.95
- GOODNIGHT, MARIE, MAY GOD HAVE MERCY ON YOUR SOUL
  by Marie Buck. 108 p. $16.95
- BOOK ABT FANTASY by Chris Sylvester. 104 p. $16.95
- NOISE IN THE FACE OF by David Buuck. 104 p. $16.95
- PARSIVAL by Steve McCaffery. 88 p. $15.95
- DEAD LETTER by Jocelyn Saidenberg. 94 p. $15.95
- THE PHOTOGRAPHER by Ariel Goldberg. 84 p. $15.95
- TOP 40 by Brandon Brown. 138 p. $15.95
- THE MEDEAD by Fiona Templeton. 314 p. $19.95
- LYRIC SEXOLOGY VOL. 1 by Trish Salah. 138 p. $15.95
- A MAMMAL OF STYLE by Kit Robinson & Ted Greenwald. 96 p. $14.95
- MOTES by Craig Dworkin. 88 p. $14.95

ROOF BOOKS are published by SEGUE FOUNDATION
300 Bowery • New York, NY 10012
For a complete list, please visit roofbooks.com

ROOF BOOKS are distributed by SMALL PRESS DISTRIBUTION
1341 Seventh Street • Berkeley, CA. 94710-1403. spdbooks.org